Balanced Budgets, Fiscal Responsibility, and the Constitution

RICHARD E. WAGNER and ROBERT D. TOLLISON, ALVIN RABUSHKA, and JOHN T. NOONAN, Jr.

This book was made possible by a grant from the Scaife Family Charitable Trusts.

CATO INSTITUTE

ISBN: 0-932790-36-4

Printed in the United States of America.

CATO INSTITUTE
224 Second St., S.E.
Washington, D.C. 20003

CONTENTS

INTRODUCTION

Much of the controversy surrounding a constitutional amendment for a balanced budget is still ill-informed. This is surprising because many of the opponents are among the better informed elements in the society. Polls indicate that the overwhelming majority of the American people consistently has favored a balanced budget amendment for as far back as the question has been asked. Yet the persons to whom pollsters turn for a representative sample do not seem to be those selected for the editorial boards of major newspapers. Time and again, editors and other opinion leaders have firmly opposed the balanced budget amendment as a simplistic and largely symbolic response to a complex question.

With few exceptions, the opponents have chosen not to come to grips with the persuasive intellectual case, such as that made by Richard Wagner and Robert Tollison, that the amendment is an attempt to repair a fundamental defect in our constitutional system. This defect arises because small, special interest groups always enjoy an organizational advantage over large, diffuse groups of citizens and taxpayers. It is economically rational for special interests to lobby for appropriations that benefit their narrow segment of society. If the costs of the program are sufficiently diffused, it is not rational for its victims to resist. This gives rise to a structural asymmetry in budgeting, one which is practically impossible to alter short of constitutional change. The weak, exploited group—the taxpayers—are more effective at holding down the level of taxes than the level of spending. Although the portion of personal income going to the federal government has risen steadily, the politically irresistible claims on spending have risen even faster. The result has been chronic deficit spending at ever-higher levels.

Rather than deal with this issue directly, opponents have largely chosen to focus upon trivializing objections. The level of public debate would be raised if they took up the intellectual challenge set out by Wagner and Tollison and reappraised the logic of our constitutional framework for budgetary policy. If so, they would discover with the authors that a budget balancing requirement will not solve all our problems. Other defects in the political process would still remain to be remedied if government is to be brought under control and a free economy maintained.

James Dale Davidson
National Taxpayers Union
August 1, 1982

A. BALANCED BUDGETS, FISCAL RESPONSIBILITY, AND THE CONSTITUTION

By Richard E. Wagner and
Robert D. Tollison

PREFACE

Thirty-one states have now called for a constitutional convention to consider an amendment that would require the federal government to balance its budget. This is only three states short of the number required by Article V of the U.S. Constitution to convene a convention. Besides this approval by 60 percent of the states, various polls have shown that between 70 and 80 percent of all Americans favor such an amendment. Only in the federal legislature—where the deficit spending originates—has the idea of a balanced budget amendment been received coolly. It is possible that Congress will not always be so reluctant. Between 1901 and 1911 thirty states called for a constitutional convention to consider the direct election of senators. Only one more state was needed at that time to convene a convention. Fearful of appearing not to be leading the nation, Congress responded in 1912 by proposing the seventeenth amendment, which was adopted in 1913. Congress may similarly overcome its reluctance to embrace the balanced budget. Whatever Congress does, however, we will surely be hearing a lot about balanced budgets in the coming months.

The balanced budget amendment raises an issue of economic principle. Some people suggest that a balanced budget amendment would be the height of fiscal folly, for it would hamstring the government's ability to use budgetary policy to promote prosperity. Others argue that a balanced budget is one necessary element in a program of fiscal responsibility, to which we must adhere if the budgetary affairs of the state are to be consistent with the promotion of our common prosperity. Besides examining this issue of economic principle, it is also important to explore some points of practice. Even though one might recognize that a balanced budget is desirable in principle, one might

3

be concerned about how this principle would be put into practice. After assessing the balanced budget amendment in terms of economic and fiscal principle, this monograph considers various issues of practice that would inform an actual balanced budget amendment.

I. FROM FISCAL RESPONSIBILITY
TO CHRONIC DEFICITS

Surpluses, Deficits, and Our Changing Budgetary History

During the century and a half before the Great Depression, budget deficits were essentially limited to times of war and recession. Budget surpluses were typical in other periods, and they were used to reduce the national debt that had accumulated during the times of war and recession.[1] Between 1795 and 1811, our national debt was reduced by nearly half, from $83.8 million to $45.2 million. Moreover, budget surpluses tended to be quite large, for they averaged about $2.5 million annually in a budget in which total expenditures averaged only about $8 million.

The War of 1812 brought deficits once again. Between 1815 and 1836, eighteen surpluses in twenty-one years had reduced the national debt from $127 million to $337,000. We experienced a major depression during 1837–43 and then, four years later, the Mexican-American War. The 1850s saw eight years of surplus, but then came the Civil War. By the end of 1865, our national debt was $2.7 billion. By the end of 1893, twenty-eight consecutive years of budget surplus had reduced the national debt to $961 million. During this period, about 25 percent of all public expenditure was devoted to debt amortization.

After the Spanish-American War, the national debt was reduced—though slowly in comparison with our earlier experience—from $1.4 billion to $1.2 billion by 1917, when we got involved in World War I. The $25.5 billion of national debt in 1918 was reduced by eleven consecutive years of surplus to

---

[1]For a brief sketch of this history, see James M. Buchanan and Richard E. Wagner, *Democracy in Deficit: The Political Legacy of Lord Keynes* (New York: Academic Press, 1977), pp. 11–14.

$16.2 billion by 1930. Then came sixteen years of deficit with the Great Depression and World War II, leaving a national debt of $169.4 billion in 1946.

While the Great Depression and World War II brought us a decade and a half of deficits, this pattern did not depart from our previous experience during recessions and wars. Between 1947 and 1960, there were seven years of surplus and seven years of deficit. With $32 billion of deficits and $31 billion of surpluses, the budget can be said to have been roughly balanced over this period. This period differed from similar periods earlier in our history in that no conscious effort was made to reduce the previously accumulated national debt, though it might also be noted that we fought a war in Korea during this time. Looking back, we can see the Truman and Eisenhower years as an interregnum that separated the former period of general opposition to budget deficits from the post-1960 period epitomized by budget deficits under all circumstances.

Since 1960, budget deficits have become a way of life. During this period we have had only one year of budget surplus, 1969, and this was only $3 billion. The remaining budgets during this two-decade period were all in deficit, and the total deficit accumulated during these two decades exceeds $400 billion. It appears that a watershed in our fiscal history was reached around 1960.

Constitutional Erosion and Chronic Budget Deficits

This shift from balanced budgets to chronic deficits occurred because of some fundamental changes in the constraints within which Congress makes its budgetary decisions. Some of these changes made money creation easier. Under the gold standard in operation before World War I, inflation would be offset by a drainage of gold that would reduce the stock of money. This would occur because prices in the inflating country would rise relative to those in other countries. Consumers would then find imports more attractive, and as they purchased more from abroad, a gold outflow would result. The pattern of U.S. monetary history after World War I was one of reducing the constraints on domestic monetary authorities. In 1933, for instance, the U.S. government prohibited American citizens' redeeming their currency for gold. The constraints on issuing paper money consequently became looser. The gold reserve standard of the postwar period did less to restrict the money-creating actions of government. However, this system was more restrictive than the purely fiduciary standard our government embraced in 1971 when President Nixon repudiated the gold convertibility of the dollar, thereby removing the last external constraint on money creation.[2] This pattern of development in our monetary order cannot be said to have directly caused our chronic deficits. However, by facilitating the creation of money, this development encouraged deficit finance, as will become clear later when we examine government borrowing and money creation.

This monetary development occurred along with an important change in the ethos within which budgetary policy had been made. For the first century and a half of our history, our budgetary policy was influenced by the prevailing belief that budget deficits were proper only during wars or recessions and that at other times some effort should be made to retire national debt through budget surpluses. This ethos can be said to have constituted an unwritten element of our Constitution.

It found widespread expression in intellectual discourse.[3] Many economists felt that budget deficits would erode a nation's capital stock, thereby reducing standards of living. They believed that in order to contribute to prosperity rather than to detract from it, government should promote the creation of capital and not its consumption. What was wise for an individual was wise for a nation as well. As Adam Smith put it in *The Wealth of Nations*, "What is prudence in the conduct of every private family, can scarce be folly in that of a great kingdom."

C. F. Bastable, one of the leading scholars of public finance during the late nineteenth and early twentieth centuries, typified

[2]See Benjamin Klein, "Our New Monetary Standard: The Measurement and Effects of Price Uncertainty, 1880–1973," *Economic Inquiry* 13 (December 1975): 461–84.

[3]See William Breit, "Starving the Leviathan: Balanced Budget Prescriptions before Keynes," in *Fiscal Responsibility in Constitutional Democracy*, ed. James M. Buchanan and Richard E. Wagner (Leiden: Martinus Nijhoff, 1978), pp. 9–24.

this period's views on budget deficits:

> Under normal conditions, there ought to be a balance between these two sides [expenditure and revenue] of financial activity. Outlay should not exceed income, . . . tax revenue ought to be kept up to the amount required to defray expenses.[4]

Bastable went on to modify this statement slightly, though tellingly:

> This general principle must, however, admit of modifications. Temporary deficits and surpluses cannot be avoided. . . . All that can be claimed is a substantial approach to a balance in the two sides of the account. The safest rule for practice is that which lays down the expedience of *estimating for a moderate surplus*, by which the possibility of a deficit will be reduced to a minimum.[5]

In other words, Bastable believed governments should aim for some budget surplus to provide a cushion for difficulties that might arise. This was the way of fiscal prudence and responsibility.

This effective "constitutional" opposition to budget deficits dissolved during the generation from President Roosevelt to President Kennedy. The old norms of responsible fiscal conduct and generally held perceptions of self-interest fell before the Keynesian onslaught that monopolized channels of public opinion during this period.[6] Budget deficits were no longer seen as a sign of irresponsible government action. Indeed, to an increasing degree, people believed that government could use deficit finance to improve the economy. Therefore, an avoidance of budget deficits, along with some effort to retire the national debt, ceased to be a *sine qua non* of fiscal conduct.

The Keynesian revolution in economic policy succeeded in creating a view that budgetary imbalance was consistent with, indeed was required for, "responsible" fiscal conduct. When unemployment became a problem, it was suggested that a budget deficit could be used to increase spending, which would

---

[4]C. F. Bastable, *Public Finance*, 3rd ed. (London: Macmillan, 1903), p. 611.

[5]Ibid. (Italics added.)

[6]On this fundamental shift in the framework of budgetary policy, see Lawrence C. Pierce, *The Politics of Fiscal Policy Formation* (Pacific Palisades, Calif.: Goodyear, 1971).

stimulate employment. Similarly, if inflation became a problem, it was suggested that a budget surplus could be used to decrease spending, which would reduce the pressure on prices. The Keynesian platform for economic management replaced the old-fashioned belief in a balanced budget with what was viewed as a new and superior principle, that of using the budget—deficits *and* surpluses—to balance the economy. This sharp shift in norms for government conduct was expressed concisely by Hugh Dalton:

> The new approach to budgetary policy owes more to Keynes than to any other man. Thus it is just that we should speak of "the Keynesian revolution." . . . We may now free ourselves from the *old and narrow conception of balancing the budget,* no matter over what period, and move towards the *new and wider conception of the budget balancing the whole economy.*[7]

[7]Hugh Dalton, *Principles of Public Finance,* 4th ed. (London: Routledge and Kegan Paul, 1954), p. 221. (Italics added.)

II. BUDGETARY POLITICS AND DEFICIT FINANCING

The Keynesian precept of using the budget to balance the economy called for a symmetry in its application. Deficits would be created when unemployment threatened, but surpluses would be created when inflation threatened. However, over the past two decades our budget deficits have occurred in good economic periods as well as in bad, and they have occurred despite repeated statements that budget surpluses were just a year or two away. Aside from the recession of 1975, the 1970s were a period of economic expansion. Unemployment was a little higher than it was in earlier times, but the standard measures of industrial production showed a general rise throughout the decade. Yet, quite unlike our experience during similar times in the past, we are plagued by deficits. As noted above, this sharp contrast with our previous history resulted from a weakening in an ethos of strong opposition to deficit finance.

In a democracy, a political bias exists in favor of deficit finance.[8] This bias remained latent until the past two decades or so, when it emerged as a force in our budgetary politics. Periodically, politicians must face a test of their incumbency. Budgetary policies can enhance or retard the likelihood of their remaining in office. Tax reductions and increases in expenditure will both generally strengthen a politician's base of support. In contrast, tax increases and reductions in expenditure will tend

---

[8]For a conceptual examination of this point, see Buchanan and Wagner, *Democracy in Deficit.* This analysis is extended to the United Kingdom in James M. Buchanan, John Burton, and Richard E. Wagner, *The Consequences of Mr. Keynes* (London: Institute of Economic Affairs, 1978). Empirical support is developed in W. Mark Crain and Robert B. Ekelund, "Deficits and Democracy," *Southern Economic Journal* 44 (April 1978): 813–28.

to weaken that base. A politician interested in using budgetary policy to strengthen his electoral support will tend to favor policies that increase expenditures and reduce taxes. Policies that reduce expenditures and increase taxes will have the contrary effect of diminishing electoral support. As compared with a balanced budget, a budget surplus will require either higher taxes or lower expenditures, or a combination of the two. Therefore, a budget surplus will tend to command less political support than a balanced budget. A budget deficit, when compared with a balanced budget, will make it possible to offer some combination of lower taxes and higher expenditures. Therefore, a budget deficit will tend to command more support than a balanced budget and *ipso facto* more support than a budget surplus. A simple consideration of these pressures shows why democracies, which are based on electoral competition, possess a political bias in favor of deficit finance.

Until the 1960s, this political bias remained latent because our political process was constrained by the prevailing ethos, the belief that deficits were a sign of fiscal irresponsibility. This ethos, in effect, made a general prohibition of budget deficits an unwritten part of our Constitution and prevented resort to deficit finance under normal circumstances. As this ethos began to weaken as a result of the Keynesian-inspired shift in the understanding of what constituted irresponsible fiscal conduct, a fundamental asymmetry developed in budgetary politics. Deficit spending came to command increasing political support. The record of the past two decades is adequate testimony on this point.

III. ECONOMIC DISRUPTION THROUGH
DEFICIT FINANCE

Capital Consumption and Deficit Finance

The political bias toward deficit finance that has developed over the past two decades contributes to both capital consumption and inflation. Within our present monetary system, budget deficits may be financed either by borrowing or by creating money, and the manner in which the deficit is financed influences the relative importance of these two consequences of capital consumption and inflation. Basically, capital consumption results when budget deficits are financed by borrowing, while inflation results when deficits are financed by money creation.

In the absence of government borrowing and money creation, capital markets would reflect the actions of individual citizens who wished to borrow or lend. Borrowing is possible only to the extent that there are people who are willing to lend. Saving provides the resources for lending. People who save relinquish their control over these resources in exchange for repayment of principal and interest at some later time. Investors, on the other hand, put these savings to productive use, hoping to be able to amortize the debt from the yield on the investment. The rate of interest indicates the rate of return to savers from lending, while it is also the price of borrowing. Consequently, the higher the rate of interest, the more people will want to save, but the less they will want to borrow. As a starting point for the subsequent discussion, we might suppose that, in the absence of government borrowing and money creation, saving and investment would be equal to $100 billion annually, with an interest rate of 8 percent.

Government borrowing to finance a budget deficit adds a new dimension to the operation of capital markets. When a federal deficit is financed through the Treasury's borrowing from private citizens, the total amount desired for borrowing will increase. To illustrate, suppose the government runs a $40 billion deficit. In addition to the desires of private citizens to borrow $100 billion, government now wishes to borrow $40 billion to finance its deficit. Yet only $100 billion has been saved, so the amount desired for loans exceeds by $40 billion the amount that can be supplied. As in any such situation of excess demand, the price of borrowing will rise because of the competition among borrowers for funds. As the rate of interest rises above 8 percent, some potential borrowers will curtail their desire for funds. This process of reduction in the amount requested in loans must continue until the excess demand for loans disappears.

The rise in the rate of interest due to this competition among borrowers does two things. As borrowing becomes more expensive, potential borrowers will reduce the amounts they wish to borrow. Private citizens might wish to borrow $100 billion at an 8 percent rate of interest, but wish to borrow only $85 billion at 9 percent. Furthermore, the return to savings will increase with the rise in the rate of interest. At a 9 percent rate of interest, people might be willing to save $105 billion. The rate of interest will continue to rise until the amount demanded in loans equals the amount supplied. Suppose the rate of interest rises to 10 percent before this equality is attained. Further, suppose the amount of saving at this higher interest rate is $110 billion. With government requiring $40 billion to finance its deficit, there will be $70 billion remaining for private borrowers. The $40 billion budget deficit will have crowded out $30 billion of private investment. As a result of the $40 billion deficit financed by borrowing, private borrowing is reduced from $100 billion to $70 billion. Saving is also increased by $10 billion because of the rise in the rate of interest.

Crowding out private borrowing will, in turn, bring about a reduction in our standard of living. This reduction can be prevented only if government borrowing replaces the private investment that was crowded out and if it is as efficient as the private investment. Studies of the economic aspects of government in recent years indicate that the productivity of government investment will generally be considerably lower than that of private investment. Moreover, government borrowing does not typically replace the private investment that is crowded out. While some private borrowing is for consumption, most of it is for investment. And while some government borrowing is for investment, most of it is for consumption. This means that budget deficits replace the creation of capital goods with the subsidization of consumption. By crowding out investment for consumption, deficit finance results in capital consumption. Capital accumulation can still take place, of course, but the amount of accumulation will be less than it would have been in the absence of the budget deficit. Because of this reduction in our stock of capital, we become less prosperous than we would otherwise have been.

Inflation and Deficit Finance

Money creation is another way of financing a budget deficit. This is as true for private citizens as it is for governments, although governments typically look upon money creation by private citizens as a crime. That there are two distinct methods of financing a budget deficit is sometimes obscured by our monetary system, which confounds them. This confounding of borrowing and money creation takes place because both require the use of government debt. It is necessary to distinguish between two kinds of borrowing. The financing of budget deficits by borrowing from private citizens is truly borrowing, as was discussed above. This same transaction, however, can also result in money creation. Which of the two takes place depends upon the action taken by the Federal Reserve Board. If the Federal Reserve System increases its ownership of Treasury debt, money creation will occur. This process of money creation is referred to as *debt monetization,* for it describes the conversion of government debt into money through the mechanics of the Federal Reserve System. Its impact is the same as if the Treasury had simply printed money to finance its excess expenditures.

The impact of budget deficits on the stock of money will depend upon Federal Reserve Board actions in regard to its ownership of government debt. Even in the absence of a budget deficit, the Federal Reserve Board can increase its ownership of outstanding government debt, thereby expanding the stock of money. And in the presence of a budget deficit, the Federal Reserve Board can keep its ownership of government debt unchanged. There is no mechanical connection between budget deficits and the stock of money, but this does not imply the absence of an actual connection between budget deficits and money creation.

In the absence of any debt monetization, budget deficits will, as explained above, place an upward pressure on interest rates and, therefore, crowd out private investment. There will be political gains from some resistance to this crowding out. Congress will choose the budget deficit because a majority of its members will believe that, in comparison with the higher taxes or lower expenditures required to balance the budget, deficits will strengthen their bases of support. The political gains from deficit finance vary in direct proportion to the degree of diffusion of the costs of budget deficits among the population. A cost of $10 billion spread over one hundred million people will generally provoke less opposition than the same cost spread over only one million people. To the extent that budget deficits are financed by genuine government borrowing, the costs of deficit finance will be concentrated upon the investors who are crowded out. In contrast, money creation will diffuse the cost among the population. Therefore, since deficit finance accompanied by money creation will diffuse the cost more generally, it will evoke less opposition than deficit finance in the absence of money creation. To the extent that congressional interests are reflected in the actions of the Federal Reserve Board, budget deficits will result in monetary expansion.[9]

The Federal Reserve Board will also reflect the interests of the financial and banking community. With respect to the financing of budget deficits, there is a strong congruence of interests between Congress and the Federal Reserve Board. Both interests

[9]On the relation between politics and the Federal Reserve Board, see Buchanan and Wagner, *Democracy in Deficit*, pp. 107–24.

will be better served by a policy that allows some debt monetization than by one that permits the process of crowding out potential investors to operate to its fullest extent. In the absence of any debt monetization, the burden of deficit finance is borne by potential borrowers and the financial community through the rise in interest rates, which crowds out private borrowing. Debt monetization will offset this process.

With debt monetization, the supply of loanable funds is no longer limited to what people save. If $10 billion is created through debt monetization, the amount of lending, continuing the above illustration, can rise to $120 billion. If the government borrows $40 billion, $80 billion will now be available for private borrowing, and the rate of interest will be, say, 9 percent. As a result of debt monetization, the budget deficit will have crowded out only $20 billion of private investment. Debt monetization is able to reduce the extent of crowding out because inflation in the stock of money is used to provide the resources necessary to finance the additional $10 billion of investment. However, money creation reduces the real value of the existing stock of money, and it is this erosion in value that provides the means for reducing the extent of crowding out.

IV. ECONOMIC INSTABILITY AND FISCAL POLICY

Economic Instability through Inflation

Money creation through debt monetization will initially generate economic expansion. The creation of money increases the spending power of those who receive the newly created money. This increased spending will create an increased demand for the output of some producers. As inventories are drawn down and bottlenecks to expansion confronted, prices will also start to rise in those areas where the added spending takes place. The process of money expansion is one in which particular areas of the economy will be favored over others, and, in consequence, some prices will rise relative to others. Employment will expand principally in areas where the new money is spent, while prices will tend to rise in those areas of the economy as well.

To some extent, the newly created money will go to finance activities supported by the government deficit. To a larger extent, in our fractional reserve system of banking, the monetary expansion will take place through credit markets as banks expand their loans. Consequently, the newly created money will, to an important degree, be used to finance investment. There will be a relative expansion in the producer goods industries, as opposed to the consumer goods industries. Instead of bringing about a uniform economic expansion, monetary expansion will bring about some change in the structure of economic activity. Since money creation takes place at particular points in the economic process, the expansion will tend to be concentrated at these points. Total spending will increase, but it will increase particularly heavily in the producer goods industries.

While this money creation initially will quicken the pace of economic activity, it also will create the conditions for a subsequent recession.[10] The pace of economic activity quickens because monetary expansion alters people's anticipations of the relative profitability of different lines of business. Anticipations of profit rise in those lines into which the new money flows. For instance, the expansion in the volume of funds available for lending will lower the price of credit, which in turn will make some lines of investment now seem profitable where they did not seem so before.

There are two types of reasons for an increase in the anticipated profitability of lines of business. One type refers to changes in a variety of real economic circumstances. Consumer preferences may change, the availability of inputs of resources or labor may change, or new technologies may be developed. In consequence of changes in such real economic conditions, the pattern of economic activity will change. There is no reason why these real changes should reverse themselves, so the new pattern will generally be a stable one. The other type of reason is changes in the creation of money and the availability of credit. However, the changes these bring about in the pattern of economic activity cannot be sustained without a continuing and accelerating injection of money into the economy.

Without this acceleration of inflation, much of the increased investment will turn out to be unprofitable. As these investments are scrapped or put to different uses, economic contraction will result. Excess capacity will arise as capital becomes unemployed. But labor will become unemployed as well. Both types of unemployment will result from the previous inflation because the money expansion will have created an artificial economic high by leading people to make investments that they would not have made otherwise. In the absence of perfect foresight, some investments will always turn out to be unprofitable. What money creation does, however, is to increase the number of such mistaken investments. As people subsequently come to

---

[10]A seminal exposition of this theme is Friedrich A. Hayek, *Prices and Production*, 2d ed. (London: Routledge and Kegan Paul, 1935). For an extensive survey of the foundations of these matters, see Gerald P. O'Driscoll, Jr., *Economics as a Coordination Problem: The Contributions of Friedrich A. Hayek* (Kansas City: Sheed Andrews and McMeel, 1977).

revise downward their estimates of profitability and to take corrective action, economic contraction will result as a necessary corrective to these previous mistakes. Thus the decision to have an inflation in the stock of money implies a simultaneous decision to have a subsequent recession.

What if the government attempts to counteract the economic contraction by further money creation? With a sufficiently strong injection of money, the contractionary forces can be offset, temporarily. But inflation cannot accelerate indefinitely. When inflation ceases, as it eventually must, contraction will result. The longer the inflation is allowed to accelerate before the recession is faced, the greater will be the distortion in prices and the pattern of investment in the economy. Consequently, the latent economic contraction will have increased. A dilemma results because attempts to resist the contraction increase the economic distortion. But resistance cannot continue indefinitely, and the longer the resistance before monetary expansion is brought under control—or even not allowed to accelerate further—the greater will be the subsequent economic contraction. Once we recognize that inflation breeds recession, we can see why it is possible to confront rising prices and unemployment at the same time. This situation, called stagflation, is a natural outgrowth of inflation; in particular, it results from attempts to resist or counteract by further monetary expansion the recession that was made necessary by the initial inflation.[11]

The Effect of Fiscal Policy

Many people have argued that requiring the government to balance its budget would interfere with the government's ability to stabilize the economy through fiscal policy. This line of argument reflects the Keynesian notion that the state can use its budget to promote economic stability, using deficits to offset unemployment and surpluses to counteract inflation. A balanced budget requirement would, it is argued, conflict with the needs of an activist fiscal policy, for such a policy can be im-

[11]On stagflation, see Gerald P. O'Driscoll, Jr. and Sudha R. Shenoy, "Inflation, Recession, and Stagflation," in *The Foundations of Modern Austrian Economics*, ed. Edwin G. Dolan (Kansas City: Sheed and Ward, 1976), pp. 185–211.

19

plemented only if government is able to resort to budget imbalance.

This argument ignores the prodeficit bias in budgetary policy in a democracy. An activist fiscal policy pursued according to Keynesian principles requires a symmetrical application. However, the politics of fiscal policy operate asymmetrically. Even if we accept the argument that fiscal policy can be used to promote economic stability, fiscal policy would not tend to be used in this manner. Budget deficits would tend to be too large, thereby providing too much expansion. And budget surpluses, if they could be found at all, would tend to be too small, thereby providing too little restraint on inflation. In other words, unemployment would be contested too strongly, while inflation would be counteracted too weakly. As a result, actual fiscal policy would have a bias toward inflation and capital consumption.

This entire approach to budget policy is based on the presumption that there is a trade-off between inflation and unemployment. Within the Phillips curve framework, more inflation implies less unemployment and vice versa.[12] A nation is depicted as facing a choice between different rates of inflation and unemployment, and the problem of policy is to choose the desired combination of the two.[13] The political bias toward deficit finance would tilt the economy toward higher inflation and lower unemployment than would result from the symmetrical application of the Keynesian norms. It would not, however, change the basic existence of a trade-off or deny the need for policy makers to make some choice between inflation and unemployment.

Within the Keynesian framework, such circumstances as stagflation are a mystery. Inflation or unemployment could be

[12]The Phillips curve comes from A. W. Phillips, "The Relation between Unemployment and the Rate of Change in Money Wage Rates in the United Kingdom, 1869–1957," *Economica* 25 (November 1958): 283–99. A survey of different perspectives on the Phillips curve is presented in Thomas M. Humphrey, "Changing Views of the Phillips Curve," *Federal Reserve Bank of Richmond, Monthly Review* 59 (July 1973): 2–13.

[13]See the development of this line of analysis in Paul A. Samuelson and Robert M. Solow, "Analytical Aspects of Anti-Inflation Policy," *American Economic Review* 50 (May 1960): 177–94.

troublesome, but according to the Keynesian system, it is impossible for an economy to be plagued by inflation, unemployment, and sluggish economic performance all at once. Therefore, the joint presence of substantial inflation and high unemployment is evidence that the Keynesian framework itself is inappropriate. The reason it is inappropriate is that it does not recognize the way inflation creates economic maladjustments that cannot be sustained without an accelerating inflation. In the absence of an accelerating inflation, recession must follow. Inflation and unemployment are *not* options, for a nation does not have the ability to choose one or the other at a particular time. Obviously, at any time there is both a rate of inflation and a rate of unemployment. These two variables are not independent of each other, as the Phillips curve framework assumes they are. Instead, inflation and unemployment are linked as cause and effect. Unemployment today results from inflation yesterday, so to speak, and today's inflation will breed tomorrow's unemployment. A failure to accept the inexorability of this sequence or an attempt to avoid it, say by increasing the rate of money creation, results in stagflation, in which case economic sluggishness comes to exist along with inflation.

Fiscal policy is simply not a tool for creating economic stability. Budget deficits cannot be used to promote economic stability. Rather, budget deficits contribute to economic instability in the future. Economic instability can result in several ways. It suffices here to note that there is an important and enduring link between monetary instability and economic instability. And monetary instability seems inherent in our present institutional order, in which money is so tightly controlled by the government.[14] Our main problem is how monetary stability can be promoted in our present political system, where the pressures for budget deficits, capital consumption, inflation, and economic instability seem so remorseless.

[14]On much of this, see Richard E. Wagner, *Politics, Business Cycles, and Economic Disruption* (New York: Center for Libertarian Studies, forthcoming).

V. CONSTITUTIONAL PRINCIPLES, BALANCED BUDGETS, AND FISCAL RESPONSIBILITY

A Constitutional Framework for Budgetary Policy

It seems clear that we would be better off with a government that balanced its budget than with one that had a budget chronically in deficit. Yet there is a strong political bias in democracies toward deficit finance. Thus there is a gulf between desirable and actual budgetary policy. The recognition of this gulf inspired the call for a balanced budget amendment to the Constitution.

Many people who agree with this diagnosis of budget deficits may nevertheless be reluctant to have a balanced budget be made a constitutional requirement. These people would prefer to rely upon Congress to return us to fiscal responsibility. This approach, they feel, would be better than imposing upon ourselves a constitutional straitjacket. Congress has been responsible for our deficits, so Congress has the ability to restore budget balance. But how reasonable is it to rely upon the normal processes of congressional decision-making? It is these very processes that have brought about our chronic deficits. The change in our monetary order from a commodity to a purely fiduciary standard, along with the deterioration of a long-standing ethos hostile to budget deficits, brought about a climate favorable to deficit finance. An ethos cannot be adopted or rejected at will, so we cannot look to some simple restoration of past attitudes. We must look toward the development of constitutional requirements to offset our chronic bouts with deficit finance.

Constitutional rules can serve an important function in preventing or curtailing outcomes that, while undesirable, might nonetheless tend to result from ordinary legislative processes. The Constitution provides the framework within which legislative action can take place. The importance of a constitutional framework can be seen by analogy with the rules of a game. In this analogy, the rules are analogous to the Constitution, the play of the game is analogous to the legislative process, and the outcome of the game is analogous to the budget that is enacted.

In a basketball game, a player on defense can improve his chances of success by holding his opponent. Yet, if all defenders played this way, the end result would be a less interesting game. All, or at least nearly all, players are worse off when holding occurs than they would be in the presence of a constitutional rule against holding. If one person holds, he can gain a relative advantage. If another person refrains from holding, he will be disadvantaged. Without a constitutional rule against holding, holding will become rampant once the players recognize its usefulness. Yet all players would be better off playing the game without holding. They cannot do so without a constitutional rule against holding.

In the theory of games, the situation in which such generally undesirable outcomes can emerge is referred to as a prisoner's dilemma. The basic idea behind the prisoner's dilemma is a simple one. It describes a situation in which each person's pursuit of his self-interest can produce an outcome that is undesirable from the perspective of all participants. The tendency to resort to deficit finance fits within this framework. A legislator will typically secure more political support through budgetary policy under deficit spending than under a balanced budget because deficit spending makes it possible to confer additional expenditure programs or tax reductions upon desired constituencies. Each legislator individually will be motivated to support deficit financing. If one legislator refrains, the deficit will not be affected, but the benefits to his particular constituents may be reduced.

Suppose a congressman voted against all spending proposals in excess of the balanced budget level. The congressman's impact on spending would be negligible, and his political support would have weakened because some of his negative votes would have been contrary to the preferences of some of his constituents. The situation is like the one that would result if one basketball player tried to refrain from holding. The overall incidence of holding would be only minutely affected, and the player's team would be disadvantaged. As with a rule against holding, the requirement of a balanced budget would redound to the benefit of all, or practically all, legislators and their constituents. A constitutional requirement of a balanced budget is one way to provide this rule.

Budget Balance and Fiscal Responsibility in a Democracy

There is a fundamental sense in which any budget must of necessity always be in balance. By the nature of double entry accounting, each debit must possess an equal credit, so that a balanced budget is a tautology. A person who earns $30,000 in one year, paying $10,000 in taxes and spending $15,000, has in this sense a balanced budget, not a budget surplus. This is because the $5,000 that is saved is as much a debit item as the amounts spent or lost in taxes. Likewise, a person who earns $30,000, pays $10,000 in taxes, and spends $25,000 also has a balanced budget. While his debits add up to $35,000, so do his credits. He has a $30,000 credit from income, but he must also have a $5,000 credit item as well, possibly from a bank loan, or perhaps from the liquidation of capital—the particular source is unimportant.

When people speak of budgetary imbalance, of surplus and deficit, they have in mind something different from this double entry tautology. Of the two situations described above, the first would be commonly considered one of budget surplus, while the second would be considered one of budget deficit. What this means is that imbalance becomes meaningful through the exclusion of certain items from consideration—like the saving and the borrowing in the above illustration. The reason for excluding certain items is largely normative. One use of a system of accounts is to provide an assessment of a set of transactions. There are three patterns of sets of transactions: one allows for reproduction over time, with neither gain nor loss; one allows for expansion; and one allows for contraction. A person who earns $30,000, pays $10,000 in taxes, and spends $20,000 would, by virtue of this set of transactions, have done nothing to influence, for good or for bad, future transactions. In contrast, when $5,000 is saved, future growth is made possible, so the saving is excluded from the budget, and the budget is considered to be in surplus. And when $5,000 is borrowed, a mortgage is placed on future transactions, so the borrowing is excluded as a normal credit item, and the budget is considered to be in deficit.

By extension of this reasoning, a government's budget must always be in balance. When we speak of surplus or deficit, we are excluding from consideration some of the credit or debit items that necessarily must be present in and implied by the set of transactions of which the budget is a description.[15] For instance, government debt or government revenues from money creation are as much a credit item as are tax revenues. Regardless of the method of finance, command over resources is transferred from private citizens to the government, and the budget is a reflection of this transfer. Expenditures indicate the amount of this transfer as reflected in the debit items on the government's account. The credit items must indicate the same amount, for they refer to the same transfer of resources. Whether expenditures are financed fully by taxation or whether to some extent they are financed by borrowing and money creation does not alter the fact that command over resources is transferred from citizens to government.

The fundamental distinction is really not so much one of balance or imbalance in the budget, but rather is one of whether the balance was achieved explicitly and openly or was achieved implicitly and secretively. Our present accounting convention, in which borrowing and money creation are treated as categorically distinct from taxes and fees, reflects the belief that taxes and fees are in some sense normal or proper, while borrowing and money creation are not. Borrowing and money

---

[15]On an application of this point to balance-of-payments accounting, see Fritz Machlup, "The Mysterious Numbers Game of Balance-of-Payments Statistics," in *International Payments, Debts, and Gold,* ed. Fritz Machlup (New York: Scribner, 1964), pp. 140–66.

creation are recognized as being expedient devices that cannot properly be looked upon as a normal part of the public finances of our nation.

There is much wisdom in the categorical difference in the treatment accorded to fees and taxes on the one hand and to borrowing and money creation on the other. While all these devices are means of transferring command over resources from citizens to government, they entail quite distinct ways of achieving this transfer. With fees and taxes, there is an explicit and open transfer of command over resources from citizens to government. It is impossible to increase the utilization of resources by government without reducing to the same extent the utilization of resources by citizens. Taxes and fees are methods of finance that openly acknowledge this necessarily balanced budget nature of government fiscal operations. With borrowing and money creation, no such openness exists. With genuine borrowing, resources appear to be transferred to government by those who buy the bonds. However, bond-holders cannot be said to bear any burden, for they are lending to the government now in exchange for a greater return in the future. It is taxpayers who bear the burden, but this burden is not assigned at the time of borrowing. While the actual tax payments to amortize the debt will not be made until some time in the future, their necessity stems from the act of borrowing. Instead of this liability being made explicit at the time of borrowing, it is left as something to be worked out when the debt is amortized some time in the future.

It is the same with money creation. When government finances its activities by creating money, it erodes the real value of the money possessed by citizens. Money creation is equivalent to a tax on money, and it is a tax that operates by debasing the value of money. A doubling of the stock of money is essentially the same thing as taxing away one-half of the money possessed by each citizen. There is, however, a fundamental difference between creating money and taxing money holdings. In the latter case, government acts openly and aboveboard, but in the former case it does not. With money creation, the essential nature of its actions is hidden from view and is, to a large extent, obscure. The view, reflected in our accounting conventions, that money creation should not be regarded as a normal credit item in the government's account, though a tax on money holdings certainly would be so regarded, reflects ultimately the view that government should normally conduct its affairs in an open manner. An argument for a balanced budget is basically an argument for truth in packaging.

There is good reason for what might be called truth in packaging in government. It has long been recognized that the effective and responsive conduct of budgetary policy in a democracy requires that politicians bear the responsibility for their budgetary choices. It is indisputable that people will generally make better choices when they bear the responsibility for the consequences of those choices than if they are able to escape that responsibility. Tax finance forces legislators to take responsibility for their budgetary decisions; if they approve a greater utilization of resources through government, they must at the same time impose the higher taxes necessary to transfer command over the resources from taxpayers to government. Borrowing or money creation weakens this responsibility, for politicians need not face up openly to the transfer of resources implied by their budgetary decisions. A balanced budget requirement would promote responsibility or accountability in budgetary decision-making.

In 1896, Knut Wicksell articulated what is perhaps the essence of fiscal wisdom.[16] Wicksell set out not only to elaborate principles for effective budgetary decision-making but also to describe a set of constitutional rules that would implement such principles. Wicksell recognized that such a constitution would need to contain several elements. One exceedingly important element for fiscal responsibility, Wicksell recognized, was that proposals for expenditures must be coupled with proposals for covering the cost. If a legislator is able to propose expenditure programs without having to make an explicit proposal to cover

[16]Knut Wicksell, *Finanztheoretische Untersuchungen* (Jena: Gustav Fischer, 1896). A large part of this book is translated as "A New Principle of Just Taxation," in *Classics in the Theory of Public Finance*, ed. Richard A. Musgrave and Alan T. Peacock (London: Macmillan, 1958), pp. 72–118.

the cost, fiscal irresponsibility will creep in because the legislator can get away with promising benefits without saying from whom the resources will be taken. Each budgetary debit necessarily has an equivalent credit that reflects the transfer of the command over resources from citizens to government. A rule that requires an open recognition of this inherently two-sided nature of government budgets promotes fiscal responsibility.

The balanced budget requirement is simply a requirement that government should make explicit the resource extractions promised by and implied in its expenditure promises. If a politician is to promise expenditure programs for his constituents, he should be asked to take responsibility for covering the cost of those programs as well. This simple point is the true meaning of the balanced budget amendment. What is wrong with requiring that people take responsibility for their actions? We expect it of ourselves—and of our children as they mature. Why should we not expect it of our politicians as well?

VI. CONTENT OF A BALANCED BUDGET AMENDMENT

A balanced budget is not some weird idea on the fringes of fiscal sanity. Quite the contrary, it is a practice that enhances sanity and responsibility in fiscal decision-making. While sound fiscal principle is on the side of a balanced budget, several aspects of a balanced budget amendment must be considered in any effort to make the transition from principle to practice. In particular, consideration must be given to the appropriate definition of the budget to be balanced, as well as to whether deficits will ever be allowed and what will be done about budget surpluses.

What "Budget" Should Be Balanced?

A balanced budget amendment would contain a clause stating something like "total outlays shall not exceed total receipts during any fiscal year." This statement seems clear enough, one might think. But there is no unambiguous meaning to the total outlays of government since there is much scope for sleight-of-hand maneuver in preparing a budget. The definition of a budget would have to address just what "budget" it is that is to be balanced.

The federal budget is a huge accounting document that details the various receipts and disbursements of the United States government. The receipts side of the federal budget is relatively simple. The biggest item is the individual income tax, a bite we all feel each month when it is withheld from our paychecks. Other federal receipts include corporation income taxes, excise taxes, social insurance taxes, and various other smaller sources of tax revenue. The expenditure side of the federal budget is quite complicated. The normal categories of expenditure go on and on, and include such well-known items as defense, transportation, health, agriculture, and research. For every gray brown building in Washington, there is an expenditure series.

The magnitude of the funds involved in these expenditures is immense—on the order of $500 million in 1979. If spacemen could walk on dollar bills, they could easily visit the distant planets by walking on the dollars the federal government spends.

The figures in the budget mask a fairly involved budgetary process through which the numerous agencies of the government obtain their operating funds. This process runs through a cycle from budget preparation by the executive branch, to review and appropriations by Congress, to agency expenditure, and, finally, to an audit of agency operations to insure conformity with the law. The essence of this process, of course, consists of the negotiations between the executive branch, including its various agencies and bureaus, and the relevant committees in Congress for budgets to finance the myriad governmental activities that we see.

The sheer magnitude of the budget and of the process whereby it is evolved make the definition of what "budget" should be balanced a very important issue. In the face of the tremendous complexity of the budget and the budgetary process, one may reasonably wonder whether the balanced budget amendment is a *practical* proposal. While we feel that budget balance is a quite practical procedure for the government to follow, there are several aspects of a definition of the budget to be balanced that must be addressed in any effort to draft a balanced budget amendment.

There are some transactions that are never included in the government's budget, yet reflect government control over the allocation of resources. Similarly, there are some borrowing operations by government-linked agencies that do not enter into the totals for national debt. These various transactions are referred to as "off-budget" items. There are several ways of assessing the significance of these items. A deficit in the regular budget of $60 billion for 1979 would be increased to the vicinity of $100 billion by inclusion of the off-budget items. Put somewhat differently, the debt associated with such items would increase the amount of the federal debt by about 30 percent.

Many of these off-budget items relate to federal activities of an essentially commercial nature. The federal government operates a large number of quite substantial commercial enterprises. These include the Tennessee Valley Authority, the Federal Housing Administration, the Federal Deposit Insurance Corporation, the Commodity Credit Corporation, and the Postal Service. According to the way the government keeps its accounts, only the net income (positive or negative) plus the capital expenditures of these enterprises, rather than their gross expenditures and revenues, enter the budget.

While it is true that the receipts of such agencies as the Tennessee Valley Authority can be balanced against their expenses, it is nonetheless appropriate to treat the gross receipts and expenditures of these commercial operations as one would treat the receipts and expenditures of any other public program. For purposes of budgetary assessment and control, there is no particular substantive difference between the Tennessee Valley Authority and related ventures on the one hand, and the regular budgetary activities of government on the other. In both cases, resources are being directed through government action. It makes little difference whether the control over resources is attained through taxes or through prices. The extent of government's command over resources is not altered by changes in the way it gains that command. The present accounting treatment of the commercial activities of the federal government buries the total costs of such activities. The balanced budget amendment would need to come to terms with the treatment of such commercial activities. The reasonable course seems to be to include all the expenditures of the commercial agencies of government in the budget that is to be balanced.

Since the budget excludes many programs, it understates the fiscal impact of government. There are a number of loan and guaranty programs that are understated in either their budgetary magnitude or their implication for the amount of government debt. A partial listing of these agencies includes the Farm Credit Administration, the Federal National Mortgage Association, the Student Loan Marketing Association, the Rural Electrification Administration, and the Pension Benefit Guaranty

Corporation. It is important that the budget come to include the money used to finance such activities and to cover their defaults so that it can reflect more accurately and adequately the government's claim on the allocation of resources.

There is an additional problem in defining the government's budget. Budgets refer to transactions that take place between two dates, typically one year apart. In many instances, legislation entails commitments in future years. For instance, social security legislation that increases benefits will increase expenditures in the future. Many of the financial problems of some of our large cities came about because public employee wage increases took the form of increases in pension benefits. A smaller immediate wage increase took place in exchange for a larger future payment. By doing this, city budgets appeared to be balanced because current revenues covered current expenditures. The explosion in future expenditure levels implied by the initial wage agreements was irrelevant to the requirement of a balanced budget. There apparently is always some way to fit within the requirements of a balanced budget today by promising even larger expenditures in the future. The only solution to this temptation is to institute a system of present value accounting in which the budget is balanced in present value terms. This would be exceedingly complex and extraordinarily arbitrary, and could in no sense be looked upon as a useful technique. All that can be said on this point is that the future obligations implied by present programs can be a source of budgetary growth, and it is important to be wary of these future items.

How Often Should the Budget Be Balanced?
We noted earlier that a balanced budget amendment would undoubtedly require a balanced budget each fiscal year. There is probably nothing essential about having the period over which balance is defined correspond to the time it takes for the earth to travel around the sun. One could easily propose shorter or longer periods, and one might reasonably wonder whether there is anything of particular importance about requiring a balanced budget on an annual basis. It could be argued that it makes little difference whether the budget is balanced over a one-year or a five-year period.

Nonetheless, we feel that such arguments ignore the basic reasons for the annual budgetary process that we presently have and to which the balanced budget amendment would apply. This process is designed to allow legislators to monitor and to control the activities of governmental agencies and their performance in carrying out the legislative mandates. Moreover, in a basic political sense, longer budgetary periods would insulate government programs from democratic controls. For example, a one-term president or a two-term member of the House of Representatives might find that he could have no impact on the budget if budgeting were done on a five-year cycle.

The reasons for annual budgeting are, therefore, related to the democratic control of the activities of governmental bureaucracies, and these reasons surely override any abstract case for budgeting over longer periods of time. Since the government conducts its business on an annual basis, this is the period of time that is pertinent to the balanced budget amendment. Moreover, the more frequently budgetary review takes place, the closer can be legislative scrutiny of bureaus and agencies. Thus annual budget balance makes both political and economic sense.

Should There Be a Separate Capital Budget?
A closely related criticism of the annual balanced budget approach concerns whether government should be allowed to issue debt in order to finance capital projects. These projects may take several years to complete and will generate output over a long period of time. Large expenditures are required to build a road in the present period, yet the benefits of the road will accrue to citizens in the indefinite future. Should not government, like a corporation, be allowed to issue debt to undertake such a project? Should not the annual budget balance rule be amended so as to separate current and capital account expenditures? It might seem as though only the current account budget should be required to be in balance. A separate capital budget could be created, with the current account budget reflecting only the amortization payments on the debt issued to finance the capital projects.

Despite the intuitive appeal this argument might have, a

separate capital budget would not be a good idea. Among other things, a separate capital budget would render the political control of government spending even more difficult. This can be seen by comparing two different instances of political choice.

In the first instance, legislators vote on building a road system and in so doing, have the option of choosing to finance the capital outlays through debt issue. For these legislators there are no present tax costs of voting in favor of the project. The fiscal costs of the program lie in the future as the debt to finance the project is amortized and paid off. Moreover, these legislators are confronted with the extremely "lumpy" decision of whether or not to build the *entire* road system, and the consequences of this decision will fall on future legislators and taxpayers. There will most certainly be a bias toward voting for such projects and toward a not too careful evaluation of the relevant costs and benefits of such programs.

In the second instance, legislators must decide on the road project under a requirement of annual budget balance. Here, the development expenditures for the project must be pay-as-you-go, so to speak, in the budgetary periods in which they are incurred, and these expenses have to be paid from current tax revenues. The bias is in the opposite direction from that in the first example. Legislators will have an incentive to scrutinize the costs and benefits of capital projects very carefully before casting their votes because present taxpayers will bear a large part of the cost of providing the road project. One might argue that such a situation would produce a bias against long-term capital projects by government. The issue would thus seem to boil down to the particular bias that one prefers—"too little" or "too much" public capital development.

However, the annual budget balance rule seems preferable because it gives political decision makers more incentive to evaluate carefully the pros and cons of public projects. Moreover, the presumption that current-period finance of capital projects would invoke a bias against such projects is not so certain as it might appear at first glance. For example, capital expenditures would be spread fairly evenly over the time that it takes to complete a project, and such projects usually take years (consider the Interstate Highway System). Each period's expenditures could be evaluated by each period's legislators. While some benefits to future taxpayers might still remain to be financed by present taxpayers, these might not be significant in practice. Indeed, a road system that is financed by current taxes over a series of years can be monitored for the feasibility of *marginal* additions more carefully than can a system financed entirely through debt issue.

Annual budget balance is, therefore, a good idea because it places useful and meaningful constraints on political choice. This is not to say that it is a *perfect* rule for the conduct of government, for there are no perfect rules for the conduct of something so massive as our government. The problem is to search for feasible, workable rules that encourage political decision makers to act as if they had good common sense. A rule of annual budget balance and careful up-front monitoring of the viability of long-term government projects seems to be the wisest course of action.

What Should Be Done with Government Surpluses?

In practice, the fiscal officers of the federal government cannot be expected to predict and plan an exactly balanced budget each year with pinpoint accuracy. To avoid deficits, then, each year's budget will probably have to aim at a small surplus. These surpluses raise several issues.

One use of budget surpluses would be to reduce the national debt. The Treasury could use its excess revenues to purchase government bonds from private citizens. If this were done, the surpluses would serve to reduce the interest-carrying cost of the debt over time. The surpluses will also make future taxpayers better off, for in the future there will be less public debt to be amortized and paid off.

A second use of budget surpluses would be to reduce taxes. While the debt retirement proposal would tend to favor future taxpayers, a tax reduction proposal would tend to favor present taxpayers. Of course, where the relevant surplus was small and resulted from planning to avoid deficits, the amount of the tax rebate would be small. Where the surplus evolved out of unusual growth in government tax revenues, the rebates would be more substantial, or, under the debt retirement proposal, more public debt could be liquidated.

There is no purely scientific way to resolve the choice between the alternative uses of government surpluses under a balanced budget regime. We tend to favor tax rebates because tax relief for the present generation of taxpayers is a paramount goal of virtually all fiscal reform groups. Indeed, since a balanced budget program that effectively constrains government would have very desirable consequences for future taxpayers in its own right, to couple such a proposal with debt retirement in effect gives a double subsidy to our children. Present tax relief for us and an effectively limited government for them seems to be a fair way to split the difference.

Could Government Ever Run a Deficit?
Surely no reasonable man would quarrel with the government's being allowed to resort to deficit finance in a period of emergency. However, some important qualifications must be attached. Since every politician tends to treat his pet issue as a national emergency, we must consider how "emergencies" will be defined for the purpose of allowing the government to issue debt.

A more restrictive voting rule would be the most effective means of defining emergencies for the purpose of making decisions about deficit finance. Under such a rule, after the president had declared an emergency, the Congress could authorize by a two-thirds vote in each house specified outlays in excess of the required budget limits. Emergencies, like treaties, would be defined by the number of votes required to authorize them. There would thus have to be a broad agreement among all legislators that a bona fide emergency existed before escape from a balanced budget amendment would be possible.

In this procedural approach to the definition of a state of emergency, the content of the emergency would not matter. An emergency would be whatever two-thirds of each house of Congress would declare it to be. An emergency could stem from a desire to fight a war; it could also stem from an unanticipated shortage of receipts. What matters is not the content but the procedure followed in circumventing the balanced budget requirement. It would also seem important to place some limit on the length of time that a declaration of emergency could remain in force. This period might be one year or two years, but it would hardly seem reasonable to have it extend for a longer period. And the time limit should be definite rather than indefinite or open-ended.

Although we can find nothing to complain about in the belief that it should take broad agreement to violate the balanced budget clause, we would, however, also make the point that in light of the size of Democratic majorities in the House and Senate in recent years, and in light of the fact that many politicians tend to view every issue as an emergency, some consideration ought to be given to a more inclusive voting rule for the definition of emergencies. The voting rule for legislative decisions has a profound impact on budgetary outcomes, and there is nothing sacred about the simple-majority rule. The primary effects of increasing the restrictiveness of the voting rule would be (1) to make legislators work harder to achieve a consensus for their proposals, and (2) to decrease the size of the minority that could be exploited (e.g., taxed for someone else's benefit) by a collective decision. Neither effect presents a problem. Legislators are handsomely paid to legislate, and we should not avoid making their work more difficult. Making it more difficult for politicians to benefit some groups at the expense of others would also be beneficial. As we shall explain a bit more fully in our final chapter, there is nothing hallowed about the simple-majority rule in *any* collective decision. It is entirely conceivable that the overall quality of collective decision-making and of public economic policy would rise appreciably if the normal voting rule for *all* public business, not just for the declaration of states of emergency, were made more restrictive.

VII. IMPLEMENTATION OF A BALANCED BUDGET AMENDMENT

It would not be too difficult to develop the specific content of a balanced budget amendment. Once this content was selected, it would still be necessary to implement the amendment. Several questions arise about making the transition from our present regime of chronic deficits to one guided by the constitutional requirement of a balanced budget. One relatively simple question is the length of time that would be allowed to elapse before the amendment would take effect. A one- or two-year period would seem sensible. However, a couple of other issues of implementation are more troublesome.

Budget Balance and State and Local Governments
Once it became clear that the forces in favor of budget balance were gathering significant political strength, various legislators at the federal level reacted by stating that the first objects of expenditure reduction would undoubtedly be federal grants to state and local governments, particularly units of government in states that were supporting the balanced budget movement. We can understand why federal politicians would issue such a thinly veiled threat. Budget balance carries many negative implications for their prerogatives of office. For example, many of their pet projects would disappear under a regime of budget balance. However, such threats illustrate the depraved level to which some federal politicians have fallen. Such threats seem equivalent to a small child's saying that he will not play with you anymore unless he can have his own way.

As a political tactic, however, the threat to cut off aid to state and local governments is probably an empty one. Above all else, Congress is a geographical battleground for public expenditures. Accordingly, the pattern of federal allocations among states results from a complicated process of vote trading among legislators, the plain talk version of which is "you scratch my back and I'll scratch yours." Within this system of allocating federal expenditures among states, it would be difficult for politicians to agree to cut off federal programs in only selected states. It would also probably be illegal. In practice, then, the threats of the federal politicians to punish states that go along with budget balance are not viable. And it is equally unlikely that the change to a balanced budget would be attained wholly by a reduction in federal payments to state and local governments.

In two senses, federal aid to state and local governments poses an interesting problem under a regime of budget balance. In one sense, the threats of the federal politicians to cut such aid may be an indication that expenditure in this area is of only marginal significance and can be easily pared back or stopped entirely. Maybe the federal legislators are right, and the best place to start reducing expenditures is in the area of federal aid to state and local governments. One suspects that this is not the case, or at least that politicians have not carefully thought through the matter of where to cut spending, so that such threats are just threats, pure and simple. But their comments do provide some food for thought about where to begin the process of reducing government.

The second sense in which federal aid to state and local governments poses an interesting issue concerns the appropriate form of federal-state economic relations under a regime of budget balance. Economists and other analysts have hashed over this issue for years, and there exists a variety of rationales for block grants, conditional grants, and so forth. We do not want to get into the issue of what form of federal assistance is the "best." Actually, Governor Reagan's statement that federal revenues returned to the states should never have been sent to Washington in the first place has much to recommend it as a program of intergovernmental aid. Under this scheme federal legislators could vote on aid allocation among the states, but as tax revenues came in, they would not be sent to Washington for the usual bureaucratic brokerage fee but could be retained and spent in the state in which they were collected. Whether this spending would be controlled by federal or state officials is an open question in this proposal, but the general drift of our argument, like Reagan's, would be to let states have full authority in the spending of these moneys.

The main point here, however, is not to advocate a specific program of intergovernmental relations but to suggest that the organization of these relations is a question of some importance that lies outside the realm of the balanced budget proposal. The primary thing to avoid in adopting a balanced budget requirement is any sort of silly, shortsighted, punitive action by federal politicians against states that seek this reform.

A final point about budget balance and intergovernmental relations is that the impulse of federal politicians to respond to budget balance by *mandating* expenditures by lower level governments must also be avoided. Mandating refers to federal agencies' practice of requiring of state and local governments certain expenditures, to be financed by state and local taxation. Mandating thus is a possible escape valve from the principle of budget balance, because federal politicians could cut back certain federal expenditures but require that they be undertaken by lower level governments. The net effect would be no change in public spending, but only a shifting of the locus of finance of these expenditures. Such escape routes must be closed off in a constitutional amendment.

The issues that some federal politicians have raised about what would happen to federal payments to state and local governments does point to a pertinent aspect of the implementation of a balanced budget amendment. Expenditures would have to be reduced relative to revenues. The strong and growing opposition to spending, on the average, more than 40 percent of one's working time to pay taxes suggests that some reduction in expenditures would be necessary. As with the two-thirds voting rule for escaping the balanced budget requirement in the case of a national emergency, the exact nature of expenditure reductions used to balance the budget is less important than the procedural constraint of budget balance that would require their reduction relative to revenues.

Budget Balance and Constitutional Choice

Many observers have expressed concern about calling a constitutional convention to consider a balanced budget amendment, and various arguments have been put forward against such an experiment in democratic decision-making. Two types of arguments have been advanced. One rests on the elitist premise that the "people" are not competent to take the processes of democracy into their own hands, even for a brief period. The other consists of fears about how such a convention might actually be conducted. Upon inspection, it becomes apparent that both types of argument rest on the flimsiest of foundations.

The concern of the elitists about a constitutional convention appears to have simple roots. In this view there are "leaders" and "followers." While it is fair game to disagree over which "leaders" should be in power at any particular time, heaven forbid that the "followers" should suddenly usurp the role of the "leaders." Only the special, hallowed few have the background and understanding that one must have to function as a productive participant in the legislative process. One form of this argument is that one must have certain special skills to be a good legislator. Legislators who are lawyers commonly think that these skills should include legal training. While there may be some merit in their position, we see many quite competent legislators who are not lawyers. It does not seem, therefore, that one would need to be a constitutional lawyer in order to be an effective legislator at a constitutional convention.

If background is not crucial, then, it would seem that the professed concerns of the elitists are simply a reflection of their fear of the consequences of a regime of budget balance. That is, they disagree with the idea of budget balance, and they endeavor to cast doubt on it by discrediting the view that a constitutional convention would be workable. Presumably, they are afraid—probably correctly so—that many of their prerogatives would vanish under a regime of budget balance. While it is normal and rational for existing politicians to try to protect their vested interests in big government, it is easy to see through such arguments, and they should be given no credibility whatsoever. It is thus easy to understand why most of the denizens of Washington do not want a constitutional convention to decide the question of budget balance. It has nothing to do with the competence of the people to legislate; it has to do with the protection of the prerogatives of those denizens.

At a substantive level, various types of consideration—fears, some might say—about a constitutional convention have been raised. A common concern is that we do not now have any Hamiltons or Madisons to guide our constitutional choices. The wisdom of 1789 appears to be lacking in 1979, and men of vision are extremely rare birds these days. But as a substantive criticism of a constitutional convention for the consideration of a balanced budget amendment, this is surely a trivial complaint. As we stressed above, one does not have to be a constitutional lawyer or scholar to appreciate the common sense of budget balance. Furthermore, expert advice is abundant, and one would think that it could be easily and amply supplied, if needed, to a present-day constitutional convention. Moreover, unlike the convention of 1789, the proposed constitutional convention for budget balance would not deal with a sweeping range of issues concerning the entire governmental process. It would focus only on budget and related reforms, rather than on a whole gamut of constitutional issues. A demand for wide-ranging expertise among the delegates to such a convention would, therefore, not be essential or crucial to the quality of the deliberations. Delegates would need only an understanding of the simple common sense basis of budget balance.

To go back to an issue raised above in a slightly different context, there may also be some genuine concern about the background of the delegates to a modern constitutional convention. These delegates would be drawn from the interested citizens of each state. In effect, they would represent a cross section of the country, and surely many state and local politicians would be elected as delegates and would play an important role. Many points of view would thus be brought to bear on the questions of fiscal reform, and, even more importantly, the level of disinterestedness among the delegates would be high. This latter condition is crucial to making long-run decisions about the health of the polity, since individuals must rise above their temporary stakes in an issue and choose a wise course of action for the future. This condition would be met at a once-and-for-all constitutional convention, since after the convention ended, the delegates would return to their normal pursuits. That is, they would have no short-run, vested interests in their decisions besides the *pro rata* benefits of controlling government through a constitutional amendment. In fact, this element of disinterestedness is a strong point in favor of fiscal reform via a constitutional convention rather than by the narrow, shortsighted, vested interests that inhabit the halls of Congress. Congress, for example, routinely repeals the legislative debt limitation each year to accommodate deficits. There is thus not much to fear from calling a constitutional convention to consider a balanced budget amendment; indeed, there is much to be gained.

The whole issue of a constitutional convention can be easily avoided. All that is necessary is for Congress to pass a balanced budget amendment for the consideration of the various state legislatures. If the present Washington politicians fear a more elemental exercise of democratic power, they can save us all time and trouble by proposing the amendment themselves. There are dangers in this route, however, dangers which make the route of a convention more reliable for achieving the desired reforms. For one thing, the present Congress might offer to balance the budget annually, thereby ostensibly obviating the need for a constitutional amendment. Such offers should be rejected, for they are binding only on the present generation of legislators. Moreover, as we mentioned previously, Congress might offer a balanced budget amendment with one hand and take it away with the other by threatening to withhold aid from the states that ultimately must decide whether to support it.

So while Congress could avoid the time and trouble of a constitutional convention by passing a budget balance proposal, our general view is that this is equivalent to putting the fox in charge of the henhouse. As a practical matter, a constitutional convention would be a viable enterprise. As an intellectual matter, it would be healthy for the people to go through the exercise of controlling the fiscal activities of government. In the process, many issues that trouble constitutional scholars—such as how a convention would be organized—could be settled, and guidelines for future constitutional revisions could be laid down. Who knows, if entrenched politicians continue on their merry ways, feathering their own nests and ignoring the more basic issues confronting us, constitutional conventions may become quite the rage. And, surely, the more practice we have at constitutional choices, the better at it we will become.

Alternative Strategies for Fiscal Reform

The balanced budget amendment, however, is only one of numerous proposals to place fiscal limitations on government in the United States. At the level of state government, state constitutions already impose numerous taxation and expenditure limitations, and numerous "sons of Proposition 13" have been proposed or are on the drawing boards of constitutional reformers. The various proposals for tax or expenditure limitation embody different *approaches* to the establishment of fiscal controls from those which we have examined here, but there is, nonetheless, a strong complementarity among the proposals since their *goal* is to control the growth of government.

The tax limitation amendment would limit *spending* by the federal government. As proposed by the National Tax Limitation Committee, a quantitative limit would be placed on the annual percentage increase in federal spending. This increase would be equal to the percentage increase in nominal gross national product during the last calendar year prior to the beginning of the same fiscal year. Moreover, if the inflation rate exceeds 3 percent for the last calendar year, the permitted percentage increase in federal spending during the subsequent fiscal year would have to be reduced by one-fourth of the percentage by which the inflation rate exceeds 3 percent.

In the absence of a balanced budget amendment, tax limitation would be likely to lead to even larger deficits and money creation in an effort to escape the tax limits. When combined with a balanced budget requirement, however, a greater measure of control over the size of government can be exercised. There is, it should be noted, one very important difference between the tax limitation approach and the balanced budget approach. The tax limitation approach makes no effort to deal with the reasons why government has become so wastefully large. It treats the symptoms rather than the cause of our troubles. It recognizes that the government is out of control but does not inquire into or attempt to correct the institutional defects that create this situation. The balanced budget approach, on the other hand, reflects an awareness that there are institutional defects that produce our difficulties with government and further reflects a desire to remedy these defects through modification of the institutional order within which budgetary decisions are made.

A balanced budget by itself is, of course, no panacea. However, the irresponsibility that is possible because the cost of government programs can be left implicit rather than made explicit is addressed and remedied by the balanced budget amendment. The balanced budget amendment represents a desirable first step in creating a set of fiscal institutions that will soften the conflict between democracy and prosperity—a conflict that has been developing over the past generation or so. We have nothing to lose by adopting the balanced budget amendment except the economic troubles that result from a set of political institutions that are not consistent with the essential requirements of fiscal and economic responsibility.

VIII. INSTITUTIONAL REQUISITES FOR A PROSPEROUS DEMOCRACY: The Steps Remaining

Our economic performance in recent times can only be described as horrendous. Over the past decade real disposable income—allowing for inflation and taxes—has declined for about 20 percent of all American families.

This horrendous performance is due to defects in our present system for making budgetary choices. The ability to promise government expenditures without at the same time making commitments for financing them is one very substantial defect. The balanced budget amendment would address this defect. But there are also other defects in our constitutional framework for making budgetary choices.

Constitutional Reform beyond Budget Balance

One other major defect is the increasing ability of smaller and smaller subsets of the legislative assembly to implement budgetary decisions. It could be remedied by requiring that budgetary decisions be made, not by a simple majority of legislators, but by some qualified majority, comprising say three-fourths or more of the legislature. The reason for this proposal is to curtail further the scope for irresponsible fiscal action. As fewer legislators are required to approve budgetary actions, it becomes easier for special interest groups to impose the cost of their programs on those who do not benefit from the programs. The simple majority vote, for instance, makes it possible to enact expenditure programs that provide moderate benefits for 51 percent of the population while imposing substantial costs on the remaining 49 percent. As a consequence, many wasteful programs can be enacted, and government can become quite bloated. As voting rules become more restrictive, the opportunity for this type of fiscal irresponsibility diminishes. However, the trend in legislative assemblies has been in the opposite direction. With the development of a large legislative agenda, committee specialization increases. With much congressional decision-making delegated to such committees, decisions come to be made by less than a majority of participants.[17] Rule by minorities comes to occur, and it becomes possible to pass legislation that imposes more costs than benefits on most citizens.

There are other defects of existing budgetary processes that cannot be addressed in this monograph. With the growth of government, power has been shifting from the legislature to the bureaucracy. There has been a substantial increase in the relative importance of the bureaucracy, whether measured by the number of government agencies per legislator, by the number of government employees per legislator, or by some other indicator. This has led to an increase in the ability of various interests to enact budgets, leading to a further reduction in the consensus required before budgetary action can be taken. The Federal Reserve System of independent monetary control is yet another defect. And there are many more, which must be remedied by strategies other than a balanced budget if government is to be brought under control.

---

[17]William A. Niskanen, "The Pathology of Politics," in *Capitalism and Freedom: Problems and Prospects,* ed. Richard T. Seldon (Charlottesville: University Press of Virginia, 1975), pp. 20–35.

APPENDIX: BUDGETARY EQUIVALENCE OF GOVERNMENT REGULATION

The balanced budget amendment is designed to restrain the growth of public expenditures, and we have argued that budget balance is a useful first step in this regard. However, government affects our lives in many ways, not all of which can be summarized in the expenditures of the various agencies of the government. Government regulation is an example. The budgets of the various regulatory agencies of the government represent an extremely small proportion of federal expenditure. As direct expenditures for resources, these agencies do not "cost" taxpayers very much. As we shall see, however, the extent of their real impact on the economy far exceeds their budgetary cost to taxpayers.

In principle, anything that can be accomplished through the taxing and spending aspects of the budget can be accomplished instead through government regulation. A war can be fought by raising taxes and using the resources to hire the necessary labor, materials, and equipment. Alternatively, it could be fought by requiring that people simply make the needed labor and resources available. Education can likewise be provided by extracting taxes and using the proceeds to hire the necessary labor and facilities. It could also be provided without budgetary outlay simply by requiring parents to see that their children receive a stipulated education. Any adjustment in the allocation of resources that can be achieved through a budget can also be achieved through a program of government regulation.

The fundamental issue that we must confront in discussing government regulation is *why* government regulates the private economy. Modern economics has two theories of government regulation. An examination of these different theories will relate to and reinforce our earlier discussions about political processes and the constraining function of constitutions.

One theoretical approach stresses the reasons why the market economy fails to function properly in allocating resources, and proposes government intervention in the private economy to regulate and to "correct" such market failures. This approach rests on the value judgment that government *can* increase social welfare by intervening in the private sector. In this view the state is a *productive* entity that produces public goods, internalizes social costs and benefits, regulates natural monopolies effectively, redistributes income to obtain social justice, and in general is an all-around good guy.[18]

The second approach to understanding government regulation is based upon a recognition that in many instances there is a sizable gap between standard economic rationalizations for government intervention in the economy and the actual instances of state intervention. While the first approach might be termed the market-failure approach, the second approach to analyzing government regulation can be called the government-failure approach. This latter approach is based on the observed imperfections of governmental "solutions" to private "problems." The government-failure approach thus stresses that the market-failure approach is flawed by the unwarranted assumption that government can be called upon to correct imperfect markets in a costless and perfect manner. We hardly need demonstrate that the state is not a perfect instrument for doing anything.

What does this government-failure approach imply for government regulation? Primarily, it leads to a rejection of the market-failure approach to understanding why government regulates the private sector. While it is nice to think of governmental agents as selfless seekers after the public interest, this is not a very useful way to discuss government regulation. A public agent will no more pursue something called the public interest, as contrasted with pursuing his or her personal interest,

---

[18]A. C. Pigou is the modern grandfather of this approach. In particular, see his *The Economics of Welfare*, 4th ed. (London: Macmillan, 1932).

than will a private agent. Public interest is an outcome of the pursuit of personal interest within a given institutional framework. Private firms in a competitive market adapt their production to the efficient satisfaction of consumer desires. They do this not from any self-effacing desire to sacrifice for consumer gain, but rather from a recognition that within a competitive institutional framework, this is the way in which they can best enhance their own prosperity. Likewise, the institutional framework of the public economy and the actions of self-interested agents in that setting serve as appropriate focal points for the analysis of government regulation.

In this analysis, what can be said about the origin of government regulation of the economy? Primarily, regulation comes about in this theory as the result of interest groups lobbying for protection from competition. The common line of analysis says that small groups of producers are able to effect a cartel through government regulation of entry and prices in their industry. This cartel operates at the expense of consumers and society generally. Producers are small enough in numbers to make the returns from lobbying exceed the costs, and despite the loss in real income that they suffer from monopoly-enhancing regulation, consumers will normally succumb to producer interests because consumers are a large and widely dispersed group that faces high costs of organizing to resist regulations in favor of producer monopoly. While this story fits some cases of government regulation (e.g., the ICC), it is too monolithic to serve as a general theory of regulation. A more general theory would stress the configuration of costs and benefits that various interest groups face for seeking wealth transfers through the state and the fact that government regulation is not monolithically oriented to favor producer interests. Indeed, some of the most powerful and effective lobbying groups are large groups of laborers, e.g., labor unions.[19]

[19]See George J. Stigler, "The Theory of Economic Regulation," *Bell Journal of Economics and Management Science* 2 (Spring 1971): 3–21; and Sam Peltzman, "Toward a More General Theory of Regulation," *Journal of Law and Economics* 2 (August 1976): 211–40, for two modern presentations of this theory of economic regulation.

However one chooses to do the analysis, the crux of this theory of government regulation is that the goal of groups who seek regulation is somehow to transfer wealth to themselves. Such activity is made possible by voter shirking. Voting is costly, and individuals will let their wealth be taken away from them so long as the costs of changing political decisions are greater than the amount of wealth taken away. Going back to our earlier discussion of voting rules and collective choice procedures, if collective decisions are easily influenced, only small amounts of wealth transfer will be allowed. As the costs of monitoring and sanctioning collective decisions rise, a larger quantity of wealth transfer via government regulation will take place.

We have now addressed the question of why government regulation exists; it exists as a means of wealth transfer to successful interest groups. These transfers are, in effect, a form of taxation. When they are combined with the associated economic costs of government regulation, their impact on the economy far exceeds the budgetary expenditures of the regulatory agencies. We turn now to a closer consideration of the nature of these costs of government regulation.

Essentially, there are two major types of cost of monopoly-inspired government regulation. The first is what conventional economics refers to as the welfare cost of monopoly. Government regulation typically restricts competition in an industry by banning both entry by outsiders and price competition by regulated producers (entry from within). These actions cause prices in the industry to rise toward a monopoly level. As prices rise above the competitive level, there are two effects in the market for the industry's output. First, some income is transferred from consumers to producers in the form of monopoly rents. This is an example of the wealth transfers that we discussed above, and we shall have more to say about it shortly. Second, as prices rise above the competitive level in the regulated industry, some consumers will refrain from purchasing the industry's product at higher prices. These consumers, who are priced out of the market, incur a loss that no one recoups. It is this loss that economists normally refer to as the welfare cost of monopoly.[20] The magnitude of this cost varies with the type and scope of government regulation of industry, and has been estimated to be in excess of $100 billion annually.

What about the other effect of higher prices due to government regulation—the transfer of income from consumers to producers? As we stressed above, producers will expand resources to lobby for these transfers. The fact that resources are employed to effect a pure transfer of wealth leads to a second cost of government regulation, which has been termed the rent-seeking cost of monopoly and regulation.

Rent-seeking may be explained by an example. An interest group hires a lawyer to represent to government officials its interest in higher prices. The worth of the higher prices to the interest group is represented by the monopoly rents inherent in the price increase. In general, then, the interest group will expend resources to capture these rents up to the value of the expected returns. However, these expenditures by the interest group to transfer income from consumers to themselves do not contribute to the real productive activity of the economy. They are merely expenditures designed to bring about a transfer of income. The cost to the economy of such rent-seeking expenditures is the value of the output that they could have produced had they been gainfully employed elsewhere. The lawyer, for example, could have been closing real estate transactions rather than seeking the transfer for the interest group. Any expenditures by an interest group to capture returns from government regulation are thus a waste from society's point of view, and represent an additional cost of monopoly and regulation to the economy.[21]

---

[20]See Arnold C. Harberger, "Monopoly and Resource Allocation," *American Economic Review* 44 (May 1954): 77–87.

[21]For the basic papers on the rent-seeking costs of monopoly and regulation, see Gordon Tullock, "The Welfare Costs of Tariffs, Monopolies, and Theft," *Western Economic Journal* 5 (June 1967): 224–32; Anne O. Krueger, "Political Economy of the Rent-Seeking Society," *American Economic Review* 64 (June 1974): 291–303; and Richard A. Posner, "The Social Cost of Monopoly and Regulation," *Journal of Political Economy* 83 (August 1975): 807–27.

In both the case of the traditional cost of monopoly and the rent-seeking cost, then, government regulation imposes significant costs on the economy. The importance of these costs for the present study is twofold. First, and perhaps most important, the regulatory activities of government are normally cloaked in the rhetoric of public interest. Politicians claim that these agencies protect consumers from the power of big business. As we hope to have demonstrated, the basic function of these agencies is to protect us from *lower* prices and a *more efficient* economy.

Second, government regulation has a massive impact on the economy, the costs of which are *not* included in the expenditure totals for government. Control of the budget, therefore, will not control the real costs of government regulation. This is a battle in the fight to control governmental activity—a battle that must be fought *in addition to* the fight to control government expenditures. Moreover, there is no easy route to the deregulation of industry. One conceivable suggestion would be a sunset law, under which all government agencies, but in particular the regulatory agencies, periodically would have to justify their continued existence or otherwise face the prospect of being put out of business. Such a law would supersede the normal budgetary process, wherein all that is at stake in any given year is the increment to next year's budget. If the regulatory bodies had to defend their total operations every five years, there might be a far more reasonable prospect of reducing their impact on the economy. However, this is simply to suggest once again that the balanced budget amendment is only a first step in the process of reform to control government. Down the road surely lies a struggle to rid ourselves of the vast tax burden placed upon us through government regulation.

B. A COMPELLING CASE
FOR A CONSTITUTIONAL AMENDMENT
TO BALANCE THE BUDGET
AND LIMIT TAXES

By Alvin Rabushka

Introduction

On November 26, 1798, a decade after the U.S. Constitution was written, Thomas Jefferson wrote, "I wish it were possible to obtain a single amendment to our Constitution. I would be willing to depend on that alone for the reduction of the administration of our government to the genuine principles of its Constitution; I mean an additional article, taking from the federal government the power of borrowing."

Today, the need for such an amendment to the Constitution is greater than ever. Large and protracted federal deficits have brought havoc to today's economy. The nation's trillion dollar debt represents a true and onerous burden to the average American citizen. The carrying cost on the debt has skyrocketed. The bill we pay arrives in several forms: higher taxes, declining real income, higher interest rates and, at present, a recession.

Are deficits the only cause of our economic troubles? Of course not. Many of the undesirable consequences popularly attributed to deficits would have occurred if government spending and money creation had followed their historic path of the past twenty years even with the budget balanced. However, the burden of taxation on current and future generations would have been quantitatively different. Government debt would be lower, tax rates higher and inflation about the same. The disincentive effect of taxes on investment and employment would not have been avoided. Therefore, in order to preserve our economic and political freedom, it's necessary both to outlaw deficits and to place a cap on taxes such that the size of government, relative to the entire economy, does not increase.

Statutory Reform: Historically and Inherently Flawed

Reforming the federal budget process has been and remains a popular topic with politicians, scholars and taxpayers. Many of the reformers believe that statutory changes in the way Congress conducts its business can bring about a responsible federal budget without resort to a constitutional amendment. Proponents of this view claim that statutory reform would avoid the time-consuming and cumbersome process of amending the Constitution to achieve fiscal restraint. They believe that Congress is capable of drafting legislation that will put its fiscal house back in order. This view has repeatedly been proven false, however.

Concern over reforming the congressional budget process has been debated extensively since 1921. For example, the Revenue Act of 1964 stated:

> To further the objective of balanced budgets in the near future, Congress by this action recognizes the importance of taking all reasonble means to restrain government spending.

The Budget and Impoundment Control Act of 1974 enacted major reforms—the establishment of budget committees within each house, the creation of the Congressional Budget Office to supply timely information and analysis, and the development of a budgetary timetable—to enable Congress to consider individual spending measures in light of overall budget objectives. In the Humphrey-Hawkins Full Employment Act, a balanced budget was declared to be a national public policy priority. An amendment offered by Rep. (now Senator) Charles Grassley and Senator Harry Byrd, Jr. to an IMF loan program measure was enacted into law and requires that, beginning with FY 1981, total budget outlays of the federal government "shall not" exceed its receipts (P.L. 95-435). In 1979, a provision in a measure to increase the public debt limit stated that "Congress shall balance the federal budget" (P.L. 96-5), which required the congressional budget committees to propose balanced budgets for FY 1981 and subsequent years.

None of these measures have effectively constrained deficits. None has reduced the share of national income taxed or spent by the government. The most obvious reason for this is that no Congress can bind a succeeding Congress by a simple statute. A balanced budget or tax limitation statute can itself be repealed by the simple expedient of adopting a new statute or new budget which is in conflict with the earlier measure. The

Byrd-Grassley amendment, which required a balanced budget for FY 1981, provided no deterrent whatsoever to the adoption of a budget with a $50 billion deficit for that year.

Indeed, legislation passed by Congress has exacerbated the problem of runaway federal spending. A convincing case can be made that control over the budget has steadily declined since the 1974 Act. Despite congressional adherence to the budget timetable, deficits have assumed record proportions: seven deficits exceeded $40 billion in the 1970s, and a regime of $100 billion deficits appears likely in the early 1980s. Control over off-budget outlays has eroded even more sharply: off-budget outlays have increased from less than $1 billion in FY 1973 to surpass $20 billion in FY 1982. Finally, those items in the budget which are known as "uncontrollable" have increased from 72 percent in FY 1973 to 77 percent in the FY 1983 budget. (Technically defined, an uncontrollable is budget authority or an outlay which would require substantive legislation to cancel. These consist chiefly of open-ended entitlements such as Social Security and Medicare, open-ended programs such as interest payments on the national debt and farm price supports, and contracts and obligations entered upon in the past and payable in the present.) Congress has thus been wholly unable to impose its own priorities on the budget.

The source of this failure lies in the fact that there is a structural bias within our political system that causes higher levels of spending, taxing, and deficits than are desired by the people, even though most members of Congress believe that large deficits and excessive government spending damage the economy. This spending bias has yet to be corrected by internal reform, because none of these reforms allow members to cope with spending pressures. As will be demonstrated, the removal of prior constraints calls for the imposition of a new constraint. A constitutional amendment would reimpose those constraints that the framers of the Constitution originally imposed or assumed. It would go a long way to correcting the serious defects in the institutional setting within which Congress now operates.

Amending the Constitution

Article V of the Constitution provides two methods of proposing amendments. The first method, by which all 26 amendments have thus far been adopted, requires the proposal of an amendment by two-thirds of each House of Congress, and ratification by three-fourths of the states. The second method allows for an amendment drawn by a constitutional convention, which must be called by Congress in response to the application of two-thirds of the states. Whichever method is invoked, the proposed amendment must be approved by three-fourths of the states (38) before it becomes part of the Constitution.

Since 1975, the National Taxpayers Union has worked with the state legislatures to pass resolutions—of which thirty-one have thus far been approved—calling upon the Congress to invoke Article V of the Constitution and convene a constitutional convention for the purpose of writing a balanced budget amendment.

In early 1979, largely because of pressure being exerted by the states to convene a constitutional convention, the Senate Judiciary Subcommittee on the Constitution also began efforts to develop its own constitutional proposal to prohibit budget deficits. Senate Joint Resolution 58 (S.J. Res. 58), a combined balanced budget-tax limitation amendment, was reported out of the full Senate Committee on the Judiciary on May 19, 1981. Its companion in the House of Representatives is House Joint Resolution 350. The National Taxpayers Union is still actively working with several state legislatures—trying to bring the constitutional convention movement to a successful conclusion—in the belief that the continued pressure from the states will force the Congress to act.

A balanced budget amendment could overcome the inherent bias for increased federal spending by restoring the link between federal spending and taxing decisions. Under the terms of S.J. Res. 58, Congress could only adopt a planned budget deficit upon a three-fifths vote of the whole membership of both Houses. Moreover, unless Congress approved a bill by a majority vote of both Houses to increase taxes, federal revenues could not grow faster than the private economy; the amendment thus prohibits the federal government from consuming an ever-increasing share of our income.

Americans have come to the realization that the problem of deficits in this country is not one that can be resolved by any one individual or group of individuals. It is an institutional problem requiring a constitutional solution.

Many Americans believed that the election of fiscal conservatives would restore integrity to the conduct of the nation's fiscal business. They believed that a conservative President, Ronald Reagan, working with a conservative Congress would get control over the federal budget process. To their dismay, President Reagan has already abandoned his goal of a balanced budget by 1984. He has proposed future budgets with all-time record deficits, and he has even presided over an overall increase in government spending as a share of Gross National Product. The national debt, which surpassed $1 trillion in October 1981, is now forecast to grow by half-a-trillion dollars by 1985.

As a result of this abysmal failure to bring deficits under control, support for a balanced budget amendment now transcends both members of Congress and the state legislatures. Despairing of the federal government's ability to restrain spending and eliminate deficits, the American public has expressed its support for a constitutional amendment to require a balanced federal budget. According to Gallup, 80 percent of all Americans favor such an amendment.

Had the founding fathers not taken for granted the concepts of limited government, they might have incorporated a balanced budget amendment into the original constitution. Indeed, it was the Sixteenth Amendment, which authorized Congress to "lay and collect taxes on incomes," that is at the root of our present discontent with the budget process. Without a progressive income tax code, government spending might be substantially lower and the need for a restraining amendment correspondingly less.

175 Years of Fiscal Prudence

The founding fathers adopted two explicit constitutional provisions and assumed a third which served to restrain spending. One reserved powers not expressly delegated to the federal government to the states and to the people. The second provided for per capita distribution among the states of taxes on income. The third, implicit, assumed that federal spending would not exceed federal revenues except in times of war or recession. All three have been abrogated or eroded by time and events, especially by the adoption of the Sixteenth Amendment (income tax) in 1913. Indeed, it is the income tax amendment that lies at the roots of the current balanced budget amendment movement.

Someone born in the post-depression era would regard deficit financing as normal budget practice. Yet until the great depression, the balanced budget, save in wartime or recession, was considered part of our "unwritten constitution." Thomas Jefferson warned that "the public debt is the greatest of dangers to be feared by a republican government" and proposed the idea of a balanced budget amendment as early as September 6, 1789. Alexander Hamilton strongly urged the repayment of national debt. Presidents John Adams, James Madison, James Monroe, John Quincy Adams and Andrew Jackson all urged avoiding public debt. A balanced budget was synonymous with sound political economy.

Until the Great Depression of the 1930s, budget deficits occurred only in times of war and recession. The budget surpluses generated in good times were invariably used to reduce the national debt these deficits produced. Historical deficits of large proportions arose during the Revolutionary War, the War of 1812, the Mexican War of 1846, and during brief recessions in the late 1830s and 1850s. In each instance, the debts were immediately reduced at the onset of peace or prosperity. Between 1795 and 1811, Congress cut the national debt nearly in half from $84 million to just over $45 million. After the War of 1812, eighteen surpluses (of 21 budgets) between 1815 and 1836 virtually eliminated the national debt. A run of 28 consecutive surpluses following the Civil War lowered the national debt from $2.7 billion to $960 million. Finally, throughout the 1920s, consecutive surpluses reduced the national debt from $24 billion to $16 billion, at the very time that major tax rate reductions were approved.

Sustained deficits first arose during the depression years of the 1930s and the war years of the early 1940s, leaving in their wake a national debt of about $170 billion. These deficits were consistent with the national experience of wartime and recession. When peace returned, deficits again disappeared. Between 1947 and 1960, seven surpluses of $31 billion roughly offset seven deficits of $32 billion. However, for the first time in American history, no effort was made to reduce the national debt.

Why the Congress Can't and Won't Control Federal Spending and Deficits

Due to the operation of the unwritten norm of budget balance, the federal government was rarely troubled by budget deficits through almost 200 years of our history. Indeed, revenues and expenditures were not incorporated into an overall official budget until 1921.

But today federal budgets are wildly out of balance. Why?

The answer lies in the political reality that budget objectives and the budget process are in direct conflict. The Congress, as a whole, is concerned with stable prices, low interest rates, and full employment, which require some check on the scope of government spending. As individuals, however, each congressman confronts pressures to increase spending. The reality of our system has shown convincingly that the collective need to control spending is no match for the pressures each individual member faces to increase it.

The tendency for federal spending to grow is clearly highlighted in historical debates on congressional reform:

> The growth of the cost of government as expressed in the increase of Federal taxation has been astounding . . . Our failure to reduce that cost has called attention to our need of the adoption of a system

which will prevent waste and extravagance with inevitable ineffi-ciency in the various departments.

Our present system cannot be conducive to economic administra-tion, as it invited increased expenditures through the perfectly natural rivalry of numerous committees and the inevitable expan-sion of departments . . . Our present system is designed to increase expenditure rather than reduce it.

Each committee in the House quite naturally is jealous of both its jurisdiction and success in legislation. It will therefore push to the limit its jurisdiction over legislation and its demand for ap-propriation that enlarges the function falling under its jurisdiction. Appropriations from the several committees become a race between or among rivals to secure funds from the Treasury rather than safeguard them . . . The pressure is for outlay.

These words stem from the various participants in the debate on the Budget and Accounting Act of 1921, not the 1974 Act! Yet they are the same misgivings articulated during the debate on the 1974 Act. And despite the 1974 Reform Act, the misgivings still remain.

The concerns they represent reflect the empirical fact that the American political process is biased toward higher levels of federal spending; levels which do not reflect the genuine will of the people on the overall size of the budget. Federal spending is skewed toward these artificially higher levels because members of Congress have powerful incentives to spend the taxpayers' money, yet they face few offsetting in-centives to watch out for the taxpayers' interests.

Spending Biases

This bias toward more spending is due, first, to what ana-lysts of government call the phenomenon of "concentrated benefits versus dispersed costs." This describes the fact that the benefits of any given spending program normally are concentrated among a small number of persons, while the costs of such a program are dispersed throughout a much larger class, the general taxpayer.

The competition between tax-spenders and tax-payers is highly unequal: it is simply not as worthwhile for an individual taxpayer to spend much time and effort to save a few dollars in taxes as it is for the spending interests to secure millions or billions of dollars for themselves. The latter intensely focuses on those few spending measures from which they derive benefit, while the individual taxpayer, who might normally be concerned about the broader impact, is less likely to organize for the purpose of defeating a particular spending measure. Spending interests are able to reward or punish legislators with their organized electoral support or opposition. Taxpayers find it more difficult to perceive their self-interest in the context of isolated pieces of legislation. Thus, whenever government programs are considered one by one, as they are in our budgetary system, there is a bias toward government growth. The result has been annual budget growth in the neighborhood of $100 billion, with even larger deficits forecast.

The explosion in federal spending is not due to the failure to elect the "right" people, it is an institutional defect. The federal budget process is inherently biased toward deficits, higher taxes, and greater government spending. The trends toward bigger government and economic instability reflect the decisions of reasonable men and women in Congress, who as individuals, cannot successfully resist the pressures they face to increase spending.

A second source of bias toward greater spending is the separation of benefits, which are short-run, from costs which are typically more long-run. The benefits of spending programs are immediate, both to the recipients and the sitting congressmen who supported them. The costs of spending programs—in the form of potentially higher future taxes, higher future inflation, higher future unemployment or higher future interest rates—will be evident only at some future time, to be borne, perhaps, by future congressmen. Since the electoral time horizon of all House members and one-third of the senators is never more than a year or two away, short-term benefits invariably take precedence over potentially long-run adverse economic effects due to higher government spending.

A third bias arises within the structure of Congress itself. The committee system, whatever its original intentions, finds members of Congress gravitating to those specific committees that allow them to serve their geographic constituencies by bringing home their "fair share." Farm state members typically serve on the agricultural committees, Western legislators on interior policy committees, urban legislators on urban policy committees, and so on. Reelection rewards those congressmen who successfully serve their constituencies, at the same time the actions of Congress as a whole damage the growth rate of the economy. The driving elements in each congressmen's calculation is protecting his turf, getting his share of the pork barrel, not transgressing his colleague's committee jurisdiction; in short, concerns about self come first. It is not in the interest of an individual congressman to give up those dollars that benefit his constituents, since that reduction will have only a modest or even insignificant effect on overall spending. The same situation fits all 535 members of Congress. Unless the entire membership can agree to limit spending, no one member or group of members dare risk their constituents' wrath by surrendering benefits that have no appreciable effect on the total size of government spending, while their colleagues, who do not forgo spending, continue to earn the support of their respective constituents. The only viable solution to this dilemma is to alter the incentives which confront members of Congress. That is, we must change the rules under which congressmen operate.

Currently, there are two major gaps in these rules which nourish Congress's spending bias and flout widely recognized customs of fiscal prudence. First, members of Congress enjoy virtually unlimited access to deficit spending. As the "unwritten" rule of budget balance has been discarded, members of Congress can vote to increase spending without a concomitant vote to increase taxes. Spending decisions have become increasingly divorced from the availability of revenues. As a result, members of Congress can satisfy the demands of particular spending interests without either reducing spending for another interest or taking political heat for raising taxes.

Rather than choose among alternative spending proposals, members jointly act to increase the deficit. The availability of deficit spending reduces the need for members to make hard political decisions by choosing among spending proposals.

A second element in the spending bias is that under our present tax system, members of Congress have access to annual, automatic tax increases. Our progressive tax code works to transfer more and more of our personal income to the government, because as individuals' incomes increase, they are taxed at progressively steeper rates. The rising share of national income paid in taxes is due to increases in real income or to inflation, a phenomenon known as "bracket creep," which has had the especially pernicious effects of raising tax burdens. In the last decade, government income tax collections have risen by about 16 percent for each 10 percent increase in personal income, largely as a result of inflation. In the last three years government receipts have outpaced inflation while average weekly earnings in private industry have fallen in real terms. Resources are being increasingly shifted from private to public hands. By trying to break even with cost of living increases, the typical wage-earner actually falls behind.

A progressive tax system allows Congress to raise taxes without having to vote an explicit increase either in tax rates or the size of the tax base. Federal income tax yields have grown about 75 percent faster than the GNP, which has allowed Congress to simultaneously collect a growing stream of revenues and enact a sequence of nominal tax cuts. Although Congress passed "tax-reform" measures in 1954, 1964, 1969, 1971, 1976, 1977, 1978, and 1981, taxes have not declined. It is only their rate of increase that has slowed. The accelerating frequency of congressional action reflects the higher rates of inflation throughout the 1970s. In each instance of tax reform, a rising trend of taxation was interrupted, but the long-run trend has been upwards.

Here again, individual congressmen confront strong incentives to do what is far from in the best interests of society.

The benefits that they must deliver to retain their office prompt congressmen to support inflationary policies which net them greater spending authority, hence the ability to meet the demands of special interest groups.

Congress has finally voted to correct inflation-generated "bracket-creep" by indexing taxes to inflation, to take effect in 1985. In that event, the progressive tax code would only transfer a greater share of personal income to government when real growth occurs. But many economists and politicians have begun to suggest repeal or postponement of the indexing provision before 1985 to prevent "a drain" on Treasury revenues, thus maintaining the automatic increase mechanism.

The Fiscal Experience Since 1960

Since 1960, these biases have yielded the current spending habits of the Congress; that is, deficits have become the accepted practice of federal budgeting. Apart from one modest surplus of $3 billion in 1969, the Congress has imposed a regime of persistent deficits. A national debt of $300 billion in fiscal year 1962 rose to $437 billion in fiscal 1972, surpassing $1 trillion in October 1981. Eight deficits in the 1970s were $400 billion or greater. Interest payments, which absorbed approximately six percent of the national budget twenty years ago, consumed about twelve percent in FY 1981. It is a figure half as large as spending for income security programs including Social Security. (Nor does this figure include the growing unfunded liability of social insurance programs and the implicit obligations of loan guarantees.)

The breakdown of the balanced budget norm fueled an explosive rise in federal spending. As recently as 1929, federal spending of $3 billion consumed only 3.1 percent of the gross national product (GNP). Since then, the federal sector has demonstrated a continuing propensity for growth, whatever the economic circumstances. In successive decades, federal spending grew to consume 10.0, 15.6, 18.5, 20.3, and 23.1 percent of GNP by 1980. In money terms, federal spending passed the $100 billion mark in 1962. A $200 billion budget was reached only 9 years later. In rapid-fire succession came $300 billion (1975), $400 billion (1977), $500 billion (1980), $600 billion (1981), with estimates of one trillion dollars by 1985.

A comprehensive picture of government spending must also include the spending totals of off-budget federal entities (e.g., Federal Financing Bank, Strategic Petroleum Reserve, Postal Service Fund, Rural Electrification and Telephone Revolving Fund, Rural Telephone Bank, U.S. Railways Association, and Synthetic Fuels Corporation). These have risen from $60 million in FY 1973 to $10 billion in FY 1978 to $21 billion in FY 1981. The Reagan administration, despite pledges to reduce off-budget outlays, even included the Strategic Petroleum Reserve as an off-budget item in its first year to lower the official budget deficit.

The growth of federal spending has carried with it an economic increase in federal tax burdens, which have risen from 15 percent of GNP in 1949 to 22 percent today. Taxpayers also face much higher marginal rates on income as inflation has pushed them into higher tax brackets. Households in the 70th percentile of taxpayers have seen their average top marginal rate rise from 20 percent in 1966 to 28 percent by 1981; for those in the 95th percentile, from 25 to 46 percent. Per capita tax receipts have nearly doubled in the past five years alone. The number of individual taxpayers paying more than 20 percent of their income to the federal government has nearly tripled in the past 15 years. Rising tax burdens, especially high marginal rates faced by many taxpayers, have eroded the incentives to work, save and invest.

Thus in sharp contrast with historical experience, the federal budget process has failed to show restraint in the post-WW II era. For the better part of 200 years, Americans held to a limited role for the federal government. Save for periods of war or recession, revenues from customs and excises were sufficient to fund those activities widely regarded as "proper" federal functions. This consensus has broken down in the last fifty years. The greater part of the current federal budget is devoted to activities not funded fifty years ago.

What It Means When Congress Orders a Deficit and the Effect It Has Upon Our Lives

The federal government can finance its deficits in three ways. It can raise taxes. It can borrow in the capital markets. Or, it can print new money. By raising taxes, the government reduces the incentives of individuals and business to work, save and invest. By borrowing, the federal government competes with private borrowers, raises the rate of interest, and ultimately crowds out private borrowing. By printing money, the government fosters inflation which, in turn, reduces investment by increasing the risk-premium on long-term investment. In recent years tax burdens and high marginal rates have risen substantially. The 1981 tax rate cut attempts to correct this problem. Without new taxation, future deficits are likely to be financed largely by borrowing or new money creation. Let us examine the effects of these two methods.

Borrowing. When the government borrows to finance its budget deficit, it has an unfair advantage in its competition with private borrowers. Since government borrowing is backed up by the "full faith and credit" of the United States government, *viz.*, the power to tax, the government gets first call on the available supply of credit. Moreover, the government will pay whatever rate of interest is required to get the funds it needs to sustain government spending. Private borrowers are not so flexible.

The price of credit—the interest rate—is determined by the intersection of the supply of and demand for credit. In the past decade, the percentage of disposable personal income that was saved fell by about half, from nearly 8 percent in 1971 to about 4 percent in 1980. As a result, total real savings have fallen, reducing the supply of new credit. At the same time, the government has sharply increased its annual demand for new credit. Total federal and federally-related borrowings have risen from $33 billion in FY 1971 to $155 billion in FY 1981. The rate of increase in government demand for credit has outpaced new savings. As in any such situation of rising demand, the price of borrowing will rise because of the competition among borrowers for limited funds. But when interest rates rise, private citizens will borrow less. Thus private borrowing is crowded out.

Borrowing to finance large deficits need not crowd out private borrowers if the supply of new savings is large enough to satisfy both public and private demands for credit. In Germany and Japan, savings rates have been from three to five times as large as in the United States, which explains why the German and Japanese governments can run substantially larger deficits as a share of GNP than the United States government, without equally adverse economic effects. The conjunction of rising credit demands and lower savings rates in the United States has driven up real interest rates to levels higher than at any period in our nation's history. To the extent that deficit finance raises real rates of interest and reduces investment in plant and equipment, we have fewer tools or machines in our old age and leave fewer tools for our children. We consume relatively more today but we are poorer and have fewer goods available tomorrow.

It is important to note that private borrowing is used disproportionately more for investment than is government borrowing. Budget deficits that are financed by borrowing mean that funds which might be used for the creation of capital goods are instead used to subsidize consumption. Deficits thus crowd out some investment in favor of greater consumption. Although some capital investment will still take place, the amount is lower than it would have been in the absence of a budget deficit.

Money Supply Growth. The inflation which began in the late 1960s has been associated with large and continuing federal deficits. Apart from Treasury borrowing, the government can also finance deficits by printing new money. This result occurs when the Federal Reserve Board (the Fed) increases its ownership of Treasury debt, which, in turn, effectively increases the amount of money and credit in circulation. This process is referred to as monetizing debt, which is largely synonymous with printing money to finance deficits.

It is technically true that there is no necessary relationship between budget deficits and money creation. The Fed can keep its ownership of government debt unchanged despite deficits, or increase its ownership of outstanding government debt in the absence of a deficit. Assume it does the former. Persistently large deficits, coupled with inadequate savings, will place upward pressure on interest rates, thereby crowding out private investment. This, in turn, leads to recession and higher unemployment. To ease these effects, the Fed can increase its ownership of Treasury debt, thereby increasing the supply of money. As the supply of loanable funds expands, other things being equal, the rate of interest will fall and fewer private borrowers will be crowded out. However, money creation reduces the real value of the existing stock of money, thus contributing to inflation.

Persistently large deficits during a period of economic recovery foster long-run inflationary fears that the Fed might monetize some portion of this debt. In the past decade, purchase of government debt by the Fed has contributed to rising inflation. Inflation, in turn, disrupts savings, investment decisions, and the prospects for economic growth. Personal savings rates fell throughout the 1970s and the average service life of capital expenditures, so vital to future increases in production efficiency, began to shorten.

Inflation puts economic stability and growth at risk; it has undercut investment and employment by increasing uncertainty over the profitability of long-run investments. This uncertainty, which is embodied in investment calculations in the form of higher risk premiums, prevents a normal package of capital projects—especially those for which the profit expectations are skewed toward the later years of the investment, eight, ten, or fifteen years in the future—from meeting acceptable financial criteria.

Reflecting increased investment risk, price earnings ratios in the stock markets have fallen to their lowest levels in two decades, largely as a consequence of the increased discount rate imposed on expected earnings growth. An inflationary environment makes it more difficult and uncertain to calculate the rate of return on new investment. Inflation not only skews rate-of-return calculations, it also acts to shift the investment pattern toward shorter-lived projects in which the uncertainty is less.

High investment risk thus blunts capital formation and the level of economic activity. It replaces the creation of long-lived capital assets with undue focus on the short run. To restore long-term investments requires a high level of business confidence, which can only be obtained by a credible and sustained reduction in long-run expectations about inflation. This implies that budget deficits must be minimized, preferably eliminated, thereby removing the consequent pressures on the monetary system of large federal deficits.

Interest rates are high because the demand for credit is high, especially on the part of the federal government. Money supply growth in recent years has been excessive, in part, because the Fed feels compelled to suppress interest rates by at least partially accommodating the excess credit requirements. Thus the prospect of multi-hundred billion dollar deficits in the next few years implies (if savings do not increase dramatically) continued crowding out and high interest rates or purchase of additional debt and a renewed inflationary spiral, which was the cause of declining business investments in the first place.

In short, deficits matter!

In fact, deficits matter in ways other than those purely economic. Yet another effect of excessive government spending has been the erosion of public confidence in government. Surveys conducted by George Gallup, Louis Harris, the Institute of Social Research at the University of Michigan, and CBS/New York Times reveal major shifts in public opinion between 1957 and 1978. The percentage of respondents who said that government wastes money rose from 46 to 80. But the number of those who said they trust Washington to do what is right most of the time declined from 75 to 34 percent!

Americans have increasingly felt the effects of inflation. Between 1958 and 1973, for example, the number of Gallup's respondents naming inflation as the nation's most important problem was always less than 20 percent. Since 1974, the percentage has ranged from a low of 25 to a high of 79. Complaints about taxes and government waste have escalated as taxpayers endured rising rates of inflation and stagnant real income. Indeed, according to Gallup, 80 percent of the American people favor a constitutional amendment to require a balanced budget.

SENATE JOINT RESOLUTION 58. A BALANCED BUDGET-TAX LIMITATION CONSTITUTIONAL AMENDMENT

Since 1979, members of the Senate Judiciary Subcommittee on the Constitution have sought to develop a "consensus" measure that would attract the support of as many proponents of a constitutional initiative as possible. Senate Joint Resolution 58, a combined balanced budget and tax limitation amendment, was voted out of the Subcommittee by a 4-0 vote on May 6, 1981, and reported out of the full Senate Committee on the Judiciary by an 11-5 vote on May 19, 1981. The measure enjoys the support of both the National Taxpayers Union, progenitor of the balanced budget constitutional convention movement, and the National Tax Limitation Committee, formerly sponsor of the Heinz-Stone spending limitation amendment.

Let us examine each section of the proposed amendment to see how it would redress the present imbalance in our budgetary process.

BALANCED BUDGET

> *Section 1.* Prior to each fiscal year, the Congress shall adopt a statement of receipts and outlays for that year in which total outlays are no greater than total receipts. The Congress may amend such statement provided revised outlays are no greater than revised receipts. Whenever three-fifths of the whole number of both Houses shall deem it necessary, Congress in such statement may provide for a specific excess of outlays over receipt by a vote directed solely to that subject. The Congress and the President shall ensure that actual outlays do not exceed the outlays set forth in such statement.

The purpose of Section 1 is two-fold. First, Congress would be required to plan to balance its budget every year. It would do so by adopting a "statement" or budget prior to the start of each year, in which planned outlays (spending) do not exceed planned receipts (revenue). Congress could violate this rule and plan for a deficit only by a three-fifths vote of the whole number of each House of Congress, not just three-fifths of those present and voting. In contrast, a simple majority could approve a budget surplus. Section 1 also mandates that actual outlays do not exceed the spending levels set forth in the approved statement or budget.

It is important to point out that the amendment establishes the basis for a *planned* balanced budget. It does not require that the budget be in *actual* balance during the course of the fiscal year. In some circumstances, actual outlays may exceed actual receipts. For example, a recession might reduce actual receipts below the level of receipts set forth in the planned statement. This is permissible under the amendment, but actual outlays could not exceed statement outlays. Deficits caused by increased spending would also not be permitted.

If circumstances warrant, the Congress may adopt an amended statement of receipts and outlays for the fiscal year (provided again that outlays do not exceed receipts) at any time during the fiscal year. An amendment statement containing a deficit would require a three-fifths vote only if such deficit was greater than the deficit in the previous statement. Thus the budget would not be "locked in" and could be changed by an explicit vote of Congress in response to changing economic conditions.

An important feature of Section 1 is that it imposes upon the Congress and the president a mandate to prevent total actual outlays, which includes both on- and off-budget items, from exceeding statement outlays. For example, should the economy perform below expectations, leading to increased spending on "entitlements" or on debt service due to higher interest rates, the Congress would be called upon *either* to increase statement outlays and approve a deficit (by a three-fifths vote), or to postpone spending programs and/or to reduce eligibility for "entitlements." To guard against the possibility that actual outlays might exceed statement outlays through unintentional and presumably modest error, an obvious remedy would be for Congress to plan a surplus of equivalent size for the next fiscal year.

The Congress is expected to adopt the most accurate estimates of receipts and outlays that it can in drafting its budget, but in all cases a congressional majority will be the final arbiter among the choice of estimates. As the fiscal year unfolds, actual receipts may or may not meet expectations. An unexpectedly more robust economy may yield receipts above statement receipts; an unexpectedly weaker economy may yield receipts below statement receipts. Either result is permissible. The amendment imposes no obligation upon the Congress to react to the flow of actual receipts during the fiscal year, only to the flow of actual outlays.

Recent years have witnessed congressional failure to adopt a budget by the October 1 date on which a new fiscal year begins. Congress has funded government operations in such instances by adopting continuing resolutions. Under the amendment, this practice would be banned. Failure to adopt a statement of receipts and outlays by the October 1 deadline would be construed as an implied adoption of a statement in which both receipts and outlays are zero. In that event, the Congress and the President would be mandated constitutionally to ensure that fiscal year outlays also would be zero. In short, the government would shut down on October 1 without prior passage of a budget by September 30.

Loans for which the federal government guarantees in whole or in part the repayment of principal and/or interest impose no funding obligation on the treasury unless and until such loans come into default and the treasury must discharge the guarantee obligation. Such a discharge is intended to be construed as an outlay in the fiscal year of discharge.

A large portion of federal spending is currently on automatic pilot. That is, spending for "entitlements" grows every year as a share of federal spending. An amendment prohibiting deficits would create a strong incentive to bring these "uncontrollables" under control, since they would compete directly with discretionary programs. At present, the automatic growth of spending on "uncontrollables" erodes the ability of Congress to impose its own priorities on the budget, which is tantamount to passing the congressional buck.

Section 1 proposes to overcome the spending bias of Congress by restoring the linkage between federal spending and taxing decisions. It does not propose to read any specific level of spending or taxing forever into the Constitution, nor does it intrude into the day-to-day decisions of the government as to how the federal dollar is allocated. It merely restores the balance between tax-spenders by constraining spending totals to available revenues.

The amendment would compel public officials to determine first what resources are available to government (see Section 2 below) and, against that constraint, choose among the many competing claims on public spending.

Under the amendment, if politicians voted new spending programs, they would have to eliminate old programs or vote to raise additional taxes. Resistance to the elimination of existing programs or to tax increases would discourage many new spending proposals, thereby eliminating the current bias toward overspending. It would end future deficits and reduce the inflationary effect of new money creation, which has in past years both financed a portion of these deficits and raised taxes via bracket creep.

Political values and perceptions are important determinants of government action. For this reason, a balanced budget amendment is especially attractive. It is easy to understand— every household understands the need for living within its means. It is also widely supported.

TAX LIMITATION

> *Section 2.* Total receipts for any fiscal year set forth in the statement adopted pursuant to this article shall not increase by a rate greater than the rate of increase in national income in the last calendar year ending before such fiscal year, unless a majority of the whole number of both Houses of Congress shall have passed a bill directed solely to approving specific additional receipts and such bill has become law.

The purpose of Section 2 is to prevent tax receipts from

growing more rapidly than the general economy, as occurs with our progressive tax code. Under the amendment, a "whole" majority of the membership of both Houses would have to vote to permit receipts to outpace general economic growth. In particular, Congress would be required to enact a bill expanding a specified tax base and/or increasing specified tax rates.

Put another way, Section 2 states that the balanced budget requirement in Section 1 should not occur at levels of receipts and outlays that consume an increasing proportion of the national economy. It attempts to achieve this result by limiting the increase in receipts for a new fiscal year to the percentage increase in the national income during the prior calendar year. If present tax laws are likely to yield revenues in excess of this limit, the Congress must modify the revenue laws to reduce anticipated receipts.

The relationship between the growth of national income during the prior calendar year and the growth of receipts during the following fiscal year provides the Congress with reasonably precise guideposts in its budgeting process. Quite accurate estimates of the growth in national income are available by mid-July prior to the beginning of the fiscal year.

Take fiscal year 1981, for example, which began October 1, 1980. The rate of increase in statement receipts for fiscal year 1981 would have been limited to the rate of increase of national income for calendar year 1979. Since national income rose 11.4 percent in 1979, statement receipts for fiscal 1981 could not have exceeded fiscal 1980 statement receipts by more than 11.4 percent. The planned increase for FY 1981 with no changes in the current tax law was set at 14.5 percent. Had the amendment been in effect, the tax law would not have produced this automatic tax increase. Taxes would have been about $16 billion or lower. To increase taxes, Congress would have had to explicitly vote for a tax increase for FY 1981.

Statement receipts may also rise by less than the proportionate increase in national income. In that event, the new lower level of receipts would then become the base for statement receipts in subsequent fiscal years, until the Congress voted a rise in allowable receipts.

Let's recapitulate how the budget process would work under the amendment. First, the Congress would determine the increase in national income during the prior calendar year. That percentage rise, in turn, would determine the maximum increase in receipts the government could collect for the coming fiscal year. If, say, national income rose 10 percent during the last calendar year, then receipts could rise by *no more than* 10 percent for the new fiscal year. Since outlays cannot exceed receipts (the budget must be balanced or in surplus), government spending could not rise by more than 10 percent. Sections 1 and 2, in conjunction, establish a *de facto* spending limit. Thus neither taxes nor spending can grow more rapidly than the economy.

The amendment permits federal spending to grow more rapidly than the economy *only* if Congress explicitly votes to allow receipts to rise more rapidly than the growth of the economy. It takes a direct vote of a constitutional majority of both Houses of Congress to permit the growth of federal spending to outpace the growth of the economy. Or, federal spending may outpace economic growth if Congress approves, by a three-fifths majority vote, a deficit in which outlays from year to year exceed economic growth rates. Thus the federal government is not hamstrung; it can meet what may be regarded as increased genuine needs of the people, if it also were prepared to vote on the record for higher taxes or deficits to finance higher spending.

WARTIME WAIVER

Section 3. The congress may waive the provisions of this article for any fiscal year in which a declaration of war is in effect.

In the event of a declaration of war, Congress has the discretionary authority to operate outside of the provisions of the amendment. Such a waiver would be on a year-to-year basis by concurrent resolution of Congress, as defined under Article 1, Section 8, of the Constitution. Congress would have to adopt annually a separate waiver for each fiscal year at issue.

BORROWING AND REPAYMENT OF DEBT

> *Section 4.* Total receipts shall include all receipts of the United States except those derived from borrowing and total outlays shall include all outlays of the United States except those for repayment of debt principal.

The purpose of Section 4 is to exclude the proceeds of debt issuance from receipts. Thus, treasury notes and bonds would not count as receipts, but as the proceeds of selling debt. Similarly, the term "outlays" is intended to include all disbursements from the Treasury of the United States, both "on-budget" and "off-budget," either directly or indirectly through federal or quasi-federal agencies created under the authority of acts of Congress. Section 4 states that funds used to repurchase or retire Federal debt would not count as outlays. Interest accrued or paid in conjunction with the debt obligation would, however, be included in outlays.

The amendment permits Congress to plan for a budgetary surplus. Those surplus receipts, subject to the increase limit of Section 2, used to repay principal—that is, retire national debt—would not be counted as outlays. Should the government fully retire the national debt, the amendment would still allow the government to plan for an annual surplus, and even accumulate reserves. Interest earned on these reserves, however, would be subject to the revenue limit. (Admittedly, it would take generations for this scenario to develop.)

DATE OF IMPLEMENTATION

> *Section 5.* This article shall take effect for the second fiscal year beginning after its ratification.

Section 5 stipulates when the amendment would take effect. If ratification were completed before September 30, 1982, the amendment would require Congress to adopt its first balanced budget statement before September 30, 1983; if ratification was completed before October 1, 1982, and before September 30, 1983, the first balanced budget adoption would be required by September 30, 1984, and so on.

SOME QUESTIONS AND ANSWERS ABOUT THE BALANCED BUDGET-TAX LIMITATION AMENDMENT

Q: Members of Congress face enormous pressures to increase spending. How would the amendment be enforced to overcome these pressures?

A: While there are no sanctions contained expressly within S.J. Res. 58 for the violation of any particular provision, the Congress and the President are expected to act in accordance with the Constitution. By establishing a focus upon two or three critical votes each year relating to the total level of taxation or the size of the deficits, in place of the present piecemeal focus on hundreds of separate spending measures, the amendment will enable the electorate to better identify those members of Congress most responsibile for higher levels of spending, taxing, and deficits, with their harmful effects on inflation, interest rates, and unemployment.

Q: So far, Congress has disregarded those statutes that call for a balanced budget. Won't the Congress also find ways to circumvent the provisions of the amendment?

A: It is important to focus on the difference between an ordinary statute and a constitutional amendment. The reason that our civil rights have survived for 200 years is because they are expressly set forth in the Constitution. Without the protection of the Constitution, it is quite likely that many of our individual freedoms would have been eroded over time. Similarly, Congress will find it more difficult to flout the constitutional requirement of budget balance and tax limitation.

Q: Isn't it improper to read economic policy into the Constitution?

A: There are several answers to this question. First, the Constitution already contains numerous items which help formulate economic policy. Among these is the Sixteenth

Amendment that made possible the income tax which has fueled rising levels of taxation and government spending. Secondly, the amendment does not dictate any given level of spending or taxing; it only overcomes the bias toward higher spending by eliminating the unlimited access to deficit spending and the availability of automatic tax increases. Under the amendment, Congress would have to vote explicitly to increase, decrease or maintain any given level of government spending. Finally, the amendment only seeks to reimpose prior constitutional limitations on deficits which constituted an "unwritten" rule of budget balance.

Q: Won't the amendment hamstring the ability of Congress to respond to urgent or genuine needs of the American people?

A: No. The amendment is automatically waived for one year in the event of a declaration of war. For other emergencies, the Congress can adopt by a three-fifths vote of the whole membership of both Houses a planned deficit, and, by a majority vote of the whole membership, higher taxes.

Q: Won't it be difficult to agree on the definition of national income and other economic concepts in the amendment?

A: No. The Congress may choose to rely on any of several measures of economic performance, so long as this economic indicator is used consistently from year to year, or that some transition period accompany the substitution of one indicator for another.

Q: S.J. Res. 58 is a balanced budget-tax limitation amendment. How does it work to limit spending?

A: First, the growth in planned receipts from the coming fiscal year cannot exceed the growth of national income for the prior calendar year. Second, the requirement that Congress adopt a "statement" in which outlays do not exceed receipts limits the rise in outlays to the growth rate of national income. Finally, since *actual* outlays cannot exceed *statement* outlays, government spending cannot grow more rapidly than the private economy.

Q: Isn't it impossible to balance the budget during the course of the fiscal year?

A: The amendment does not impose a requirement of actual balance during the fiscal year, only the adoption of a *planned* balanced budget. Although the amendment monitors the flow of actual outlays to insure that actual outlays do not exceed those set forth in the budget statement, actual receipts may exceed or fall below the level set forth in the statement. The amendment imposes no requirement that Congress react to the actual flow of receipts, only to the actual flow of outlays.

Q: Won't Congress just shift more and more of its spending policies "off-budget"?

A: No. Budget outlays include both "on" and "off-budget" items. Section 4 states, "Total outlays shall include all outlays of the United States except for repayment of debt principal."

NOTE ON ADDITIONAL READING

For a detailed statement on the legislative history of the Amendment and definitions of its terms and provisions, see the official Committee report: "Balanced Budget-Tax Limitation Constitutional Amendment," *Report to the Committee on the Judiciary,* United States Senate, 97th Congress, 1st Session, Report no. 97-151, Washington, D.C.: U.S. Government Printing Office, 1981.

C. THE BALANCED BUDGET—
THE STATES CALL FOR A CONVENTION

By John T. Noonan, Jr.

Introduction

One of the great American innovations at the founding of our Republic was a Constitution which could be amended. At the time "it was heresy to suggest the possibility of change in governments divinely established and ensured."[1] To provide in the written instrument itself for change was to take the position in advance that experience would show defects, that change would sometimes be desirable and good, and that the people of the next generation or the twelfth generation later could be as wise and trustworthy as the Founding Fathers themselves.

Thirty-one states have now called for a Convention to amend the Constitution of the United States to require, except in time of true emergency, a balanced federal budget. Is amendment by Convention workable? Is it wise? Are the calls by the states valid, so that Congress must bring a Convention into being when three more states join the present thirty-one? Those who are hostile to the requirement of a federal budget have attempted to cast doubt on the calls made by the states and even on the process of amendment by Convention. The thirty-one calls, however, are entirely valid. The Convention method of amendment is established by the Constitution itself. It has been approved by our wisest statesmen. The doubts raised against the calls and the method are baseless. A demonstration of their baselessness requires a more particular examination.

The Convention Method

One of the great recognized defects of the Articles of Confederation which preceded the Constitution was their failure to provide for amendment. One of the first subjects put before the Constitutional Convention when it met in Philadelphia in 1787 was a provision for the future amendment of the Constitution that was then being made.[2] The delegates—who included such

[1] Charles E. Merriam, *The Written Constitution and the Unwritten Attitude* (New York, 1931), p. 6.

[2] Max Farrand, ed., *The Records of the Federal Convention of 1787* (New Haven, 1911), Vol. 1, p. 22. (Madison's journal, May 20, 1787).

men as George Washington, Alexander Hamilton, James Madison, and Benjamin Franklin—unanimously agreed that amendment must be built into the document.[3] From the beginning it was accepted as a fundamental American principle that our Constitution could be changed by the peaceful methods given in the Constitution itself.

Two methods of amendment were provided. One was dependent on the initiative of Congress, the other on the initiative of the states. The methods were intended to be parallel ways of changing the Constitution. In Madison's words in *The Federalist* the Article on Amendements "equally enables the general and the State governments to originate the amendment of errors."[4] It was recognized that those in power in the national government might be disinclined to give up any of their prerogatives, so that it was particularly necessary to leave open the initiative of the states. As Hamilton pointed out in his Final Plea for Ratification in *The Federalist,* the second method of Amendment was provided in order that Congress would be under a "peremptory" duty to call a Convention when two-thirds of the states made application for one.[5]

Doomsayers now claim that the second method of amendment provided by Article V of the Constitution is unworkable; that it is "shrouded in legal mystery of the most fundamental sort," that it is full of "fundamental uncertainties," that it will lead to confrontations between branches of government of "nightmarish dimensions," and that its invocation will lead to trauma for the country. It is clear that most of these doomsayers are opponents of the balanced budget amendment itself. Like Charles Black of Yale Law School, they frankly admit their bias. In the 1960's when there was "opportunity to deal with the sensitive constitutional issues objectively," the view of such constitutional lawyers as Senator Sam Ervin was that the

[3]*Ibid.,* Vol. 1, p. 203, (Madison's journal, June 11, 1787).

[4]*The Federalist,* number 43.

[5]*Ibid.,* number 85.

Convention method was eminently sensible and practicable.[6]

Reading the current prophecies of gloom, one is reminded of what an inveterate Tory might have pronounced in 1789 as our new Constitution was launched. Every word—legal mystery, fundamental incertitudes, confrontations between branches of government—could have been used and would in some sense have been true; but what distrust of popular government it would have been to act on such gloomy guesses! What distrust it shows today both in the wisdom of the Founding Fathers who gave us Article V and in ourselves to predict that we cannot safely use the second great mode of amendment offered by our Constitution.

The principal objection offered to the Convention method is that a convention may be a runaway body enacting amendments on all kinds of matters not within its call. In the most flamboyant expositions of this danger it is even suggested that the Convention could repeal the Bill of Rights. Is there anything at all to such fears? The language of the Constitution is clear. Congress is to call a Convention on the application of the legislatures of the states. Congress is not free to call a Convention at its pleasure. It can only act upon the states' application; and if Congress can only act upon their application it cannot go beyond the purpose for which the states have applied.

The states which have called for a Convention on a balanced budget have been remarkably clear in what they have required. For example, many have called for a Convention "for the sole and exclusive purpose" of proposing a balanced budget amendment. Others have provided that their applications shall be deemed null and void if the Convention fails to be limited to the "specific and exclusive purpose" of proposing such an

---

[6]Compare Charles L. Black, Jr., "Amendment by National Constitutional Convention: A Letter to a Senator," *Oklahoma Law Review* 32 (1979) 3, p. 644 with Sam J. Ervin, Jr., "Proposed Legislation to Implement the Convention Method of Amending the Constitution," *Michigan Law Review* 66 (1968) 5, p. 894. For examples of doomsaying, see Laurence H. Tribe, "Issues Raised by Requesting Congress to Call a Constitutional Convention to Propose a Balanced Budget Amendment," *Pacific Law Journal* 10 (1979) 2, pp. 627-629.

amendment. If the Convention were not called for this purpose such resolutions of the states would simply self-destruct.[7]

If the states apply for a Convention on a balanced budget Congress must call a Convention on a balanced budget. It cannot at its pleasure enlarge the topic. Nor can the Convention go beyond what Congress has specified in the call. The Convention's powers are derived from Article V and they cannot exceed what Article V specifies. The Convention meets at the call of Congress on the subject which the states have set out and for which Congress has called the Convention.[8]

The Intention of the Founding Fathers

On the very day—indeed minutes after—Article V was adopted by the framers with only two states (Connecticut and New Jersey) opposing, there were participants—John Randolph and George Mason—who wanted another general Convention but showed no appreciation of the fact that the Constitution gave them means of getting one. And their chief opponent, Charles Pinckney, who had voted for Article V, was adamantly opposed to a new general Convention in which "confusion and contrariety" would result. If all that Article V gave to the states was such a power of requiring a general Convention, how strange it was that persons so sensitive to a general Convention's dangers so readily agreed to Article V![9]

James Madison had first suggested that it would be Congress, not a Convention, which would have power to propose

---

[7]See Walter E. Dellinger, "Who Controls A Constitutional Convention?—A Response," *Duke Law Journal* (1979) 4, p. 1001. See also 125 *Congressional Record* S 1306-S 1309 (February 8, 1979).

[8]See the conclusions of the Special Constitutional Convention Study Committee of the American Bar Association, *Amendment of the Constitution* (1974), p. 17. Among the members of this committee reaching this unanimous conclusion were Judge Sarah Hughes of the Federal District Court and Dean Albert Sacks of Harvard Law School. The same conclusion is reached by Professor Paul G. Kauper of the University of Michigan Law School, "The Alternative Amendment Process: Some Observations," *Michigan Law Review* 64 (1968) 5, p. 912. Also see Note, "Proposed Legislation on the Convention Method of Amending the United States Constitution," *Harvard Law Review* 85 (1974) 8, p. 1629.

[9]Farrand, *Op. Cit.,* Vol. 2, pp. 630-631.

an amendment on application of two-thirds of the state legislatures. Madison's proposal was objected to by George Mason, who thought it gave Congress too much control, and by Roger Sherman who feared that the amending process could be used to deprive states of their equality in the Senate or affect slavery in the states. Sherman's point on the Senate was met by a specific provision eliminating this specific topic from the amending process, while a similar effort to immunize another specific subject, slavery, from change was voted down. Mason's difficulty, that Congress had too much control, was met by language that Gouverneur Morris and Elbridge Gerry introduced "to require a Convention on application of 2/3 of the states." This language made the states more able to act, not less.[10]

This understanding of Article V of the Constitution is confirmed by both Madison and Hamilton. Madison says explicitly that the national and state governments have equal powers of amendment.[11] It is obvious that the powers are very unequal if the national government can propose individual amendments but the states can only propose amendments of the whole Constitution. If Congress can propose one amendment at a time, so can the states. Hamilton is, if anything, even more explicit. He says in so many words that every amendment

> would be a single proposition and might be forwarded singly. There would then be no necessity for management or compromise, in relation to any other point—no giving or taking. The will of the requisite number would at once bring the matter to a decisive issue. And consequently, whenever nine, or rather ten States, were united in the desire of a particular amendment that amendment must infallibly take place.[12]

There is absolutely nothing in this authoritative exposition that suggests that the states can only call a general convention where the whole Constitution will be on the table to be bar-

[10] *Ibid.,* Vol. 2, pp. 559-629.

[11] *The Federalist,* number 43.

[12] *Ibid.,* number 85.

gained over. As Senator Sam Ervin has observed, such a construction "would effectively destroy the powers of the States to originate the amendment of errors pointed out by experience."[13] What is contemplated and assured by Article V is entirely different: two-thirds of the states agree on an amendment and "that amendment must infallibly take place."[14]

The Locks on the Convention

The Convention is confined by multiple locks which are ample to keep it within bounds. The first lock is that Congress calls the Convention. It can specify the topic. When Congress calls a Convention on a balanced budget, it will lock the Convention into consideration of that subject. But suppose, the fearful doomsayer persists, the Convention disobeys. Suppose that like lawless judges the Convention takes the law into its own hands and acts on subjects Congress had not entrusted to it. What then? Then Congress applies the second lock. Under Article V, Congress alone can send an amendment to the States for ratification. If the Convention is disobedient, Congress will lock it into disobedience. It will not send out the amendment for ratification.

Yet suppose—a questioner may persist like a small child—Congress fails to abide by its own rules. Suppose it caves in to the Convention. The most sensible answer to this supposition is that if you don't trust Congress here, you don't trust the amendment process in any form. After all, at any time Congress can pose any number of amendments and send them to the states. It doesn't have to wait for a Convention. So one is either afraid of Congress proposing amendments under the first mode of amending permitted by Article V or one is not afraid of Congress standing up to a Convention which has overstepped its mandate.

And there is more. If a childlike fear of Congress is to be

[13]Ervin, *Op. Cit.*, p. 883.

[14]*The Federalist*, number 85. See also Philip Kurland, Statement, in *Federal Constitutional Convention: Hearings on S. 2307 Before the Subcommittee on Separation of Powers*, Committee on the Judiciary, 90th Cong., 1st Sess. 1967, p. 233.

indulged, there are still the states. Three-quarters of these must approve any amendment. Suppose a runaway Convention. Suppose an irresponsible Congress. Will three-quarters of the states be irresponsible too? Only if we wish to frighten ourselves with bogeymen will we indulge in this fantasy.

As was said long ago by a contemporary of the original Constitution, George St. Tucker, "Nor is there any reason to fear that this provision in the Constitution will produce any degree of instability in the government. The mode both of originating and ratifying amendments (in either mode in which the Constitution directs) must necessarily be attended with such obstacles and delays as must prove a sufficient bar against light or frequent innovations."[15]

Obstacles and delays do abound. To obtain an amendment by the Convention route, it must be sought by two-thirds of the states, proposed to a Convention called for that purpose by Congress, adopted by the Convention, sent out by the Congress to the states, and ratified by three-quarters of the states. To a reasonable mind, this process assures such "obstacles and delays" that there is a sufficient bar to any runaway actions by a Convention, sufficient security against all genuine risks, enough locks—double or triple locks—to prevent rash, willful, lawless action on subjects beyond the scope of the congressional call to a Convention.

The Usefulness of the Convention Method

The usefulness of the states' application for a Convention may be doubted because in fact a Convention has never been called. Is application for a convention merely a way for a state legislature to blow off steam, harmlessly, without effect? In the almost two hundred years of our constitutional history there have been over 300 such applications by the states. Every

---

[15]George St. Tucker, ed. William Blackstone, *Commentaries on the Laws of England,* I, Appendix 371-372, quoted with approval in Joseph Story, *Commentaries on the Constitution of the United States,* ed. Thomas M. Cooley, (Boston, 1873), Sec. 1831.

state has made at least one.[16] No doubt some of the applications were fulminations in the air without result. But at least three of the topics addressed by application were made the subjects of amendments by Congress—the limitations of presidential tenure to two terms; the repeal of Prohibition; and the direct election of senators. It is fair to say that in each case the expression of the will of the states for a Convention was a factor contributing to congressional action; and that in the case of the direct election of senators the application for a Convention was a critical factor.[17]

For a decade Congress had refused to amend the Constitution to take from the state legislatures the power to elect senators. The reform threatened a power bloc in the Senate. The House had proposed the amendment several times. But the Senate each time killed it by referral to a committee. In 1906, twelve states met and planned concerted action to apply for a Convention.[18] The number of states calling for a Convention rapidly mounted toward the requisite number for action. In 1911 the proponents of reform laid the states' petitions before the Senate. It was at this junction that Senator Heyburn of Idaho opined that a Convention could "repeal every section" of the Constitution. Heyburn was one of the diehard reactionaries, trying to scare off the needed change. But by 1911 thirty states had applied for a Convention on direct election. In 1912 the retrograde Senate surrendered and Congress proposed the Seventeenth Amendment.

The lessons are clear: A reform that strikes at the power of Congress may only be adopted if effective pressure is generated by the states. The way of generating effective pressure is the way provided by the Founding Fathers—application by the legislatures of the states for a Convention.

[16]ABA Committee Report, *Op. Cit.*, p. 78.

[17]Edward S. Corwin and Mary Louise Ramsey, "The Constitutional Law of Constitutional Amendment," *Notre Dame Lawyer* 26 (1951) 2, p. 196.

[18]ABA Committee Report, Op. Cit., p. 72.

The Wisdom of the Convention Method

It has been claimed that it would "trivialize" the Constitution to propose an amendment requiring a balanced budget.[19] It is surprising that such a basic limitation on governmental power should be viewed as trivial. No one, presumably, regards the Sixteenth Amendment as setting up a trivial tax. It is very hard to understand how an amendment dealing with the limits of governmental expenditures is more trivial than an amendment granting one form of taxing power. It is evident to most people that the limits of government finance are fundamental to the economic stability of the nation and are as properly a subject of constitutional concern as any specific form of taxation.

Moreover, it is a misdescription to describe the balanced budget amendment as merely economic. At the heart of the amendment is the desire to restore balance to our governmental system. A balance of power as much as a balance of finances will be achieved by an amendment.

There has been a claim that a Convention would cause national trauma.[20] In that warning I hear the voices of those supremely content with the federal establishment as it exists, who, if they do not believe the Constitution is divinely established, at least have for the federal bureaucracy sentiments of satisfaction which they do not want disturbed by any democratic action of the people. To them the best answer, perhaps, lies in the words Abraham Lincoln delivered in his First Inaugural Address at a time of grave national peril:

> I fully recognize the rightful authority of the people over the whole subject [amendment of the Constitution], to be exercised in either of the modes prescribed in the instrument itself, and I should, under existing circumstances, favor rather than oppose a fair opportunity being afforded the people to act upon it. I will venture to add that to me the Convention seems preferable, in that it allows amendments to originate with the people themselves; instead of only permitting them to take or reject propositions originated by others, not

[19]Tribe, *Op. Cit.,* p. 627.
[20]*Ibid.,* p. 634.

especially chosen for the purpose, and which might not be precisely such as they would wish to accept or refuse . . .[21]

A method sanctioned by Hamilton, by Franklin, by Madison, by Lincoln and by Washington and by all the makers of the Constitution and invoked from time to time by every state is indeed a workable, useful, and wise way of keeping our Constitution a living instrument of the people.

The Validity of the Calls

Article V specifies that Congress shall call a Convention "on the Application of Legislatures of two-thirds of the several States." Now to be considered are the validity of the calls made to this date for a Convention to propose a balanced budget amendment; and first to be considered is the forum in which validity should be determined.

The forum. According to the principal case on the amending process, *Coleman v. Miller,* Congress is the constitutionally-authorized body to decide the validity of the state calls. In this case, where the validity of Kansas' ratification of the proposed Child Labor Amendment was at issue, the opinion of the Court by Chief Justice Hughes held that ratification was "a political question pertaining to the political departments, with the ultimate authority in the Congress in the exercise of its control over the promulgation of the adoption of the amendment."[22] Concurring opinions by Justices Black and Frankfurter, joined by Justices Roberts and Douglas were even stronger. Justice Black wrote,

> Undivided control of that process has been given exclusively by the Article exclusively and completely to Congress. The process itself is 'political' in its entirety, from submission until an amendment becomes part of the Constitution, and is not subject to judicial guidance, control, or interference at any point.[23]

---

[21]Abraham Lincoln, "First Inaugural Address, March 4, 1861," *The Collected Works of Abraham Lincoln,* Roy P. Basler, ed. (New Brunswick, 1953), p. 269.

[22]*Coleman v. Miller* 307 U.S. 433 (1939) at 450.

[23]*Ibid.,* p. 459.

Justice Frankfurter wrote that it

> was not for courts to meddle with matters that required no subtlety to be identified as political issues, and the political issues involved in ratification were of this kind.[24]

Most recent cases, not specifically on Article V but on "political questions," have not changed the conclusion reached in *Coleman*. Thus, for example, in *Baker v. Carr* among the characteristics of "political questions" which the Court does not decide are "a textually demonstrable constitutional commitment of the issue to a coordinate political department" (surely the case of Article V's commitment of the amending process to Congress) and the "impossibility of a court's undertaking independent resolution without expressing lack of the respect due coordinate branches of government" (again, a criterion excluding the Court if Congress has acted).[25] Similarly, in *Powell v. McCormack,* the Court focused on the criterion provided by the text of the Constitution.[26] Hence, although both the *Baker* and *Powell* cases show the Court taking up matters that were arguably political, they have reinforced rather than impaired the holding of *Coleman* that Congress is the judge.[27]

As Archibald Cox has said in another context, discussing the superiority of Congress to Court in protecting the Fourteenth Amendment rights, "the fundamental basis for legislative action is the knowledge, experience, and judgment of the people's representatives."[28] If there was ever a political topic on which the knowledge, experience and judgment of the people's representatives was peculiarly valuable, it is what the great popular process of amending the Constitution requires. It is

---

[24]*Ibid.,* p. 460.

[25]*Baker v. Carr* 369 U.S. 186 (1962) at 217.

[26]*Powell v. McCormack* 395 U.S. 486 (1969) at 548.

[27]Compare William H. White, Note, "Article V: Political Questions and Sensible Answers," *Texas Law Review* 57 (1979) 7, pp. 1263-1265.

[28]Archibald Cox, "Foreword: Constitutional Adjudication and the Promotion of Human Rights." *Harvard Law Review* 80 (1966) 1, p. 105.

reasonable to conclude that the first and last judge of the validity of the calls of the states will be Congress.

This conclusion is of importance in determining their validity because it is fair to say that the judgment of Congress will be less technical and more commonsensical than a judicial judgment might be. Even such a foe of a Convention as Professor Gunther concedes that the validity of the calls should not be decided in a hairsplitting way. "[W]hat could do more," he writes, "to reinforce the feeling of distrust of Washington that underlies the balanced budget campaign than to have Congress strike, one by one, the applications before it, on various technicalities?"[29] It is a fair assumption that Congress, recognizing that what is at stake is a popular process of overcoming deficiencies and correcting grievances, will judge in a way which will not impede the process but will help to make it work.

Time Limits. The first question Congress must address is whether any calls have lapsed. Mississippi's was issued in 1975.[30] Will it be good after seven years? Congress has the power to fix seven years as a period in which ratification must occur, as it did in proposing the Prohibition Amendment, and the Supreme Court has observed that this period was reasonable in order that approval of an amendment be relatively contemporaneous in the approving states.[31] Nonetheless, the Court has also noted that it is within the province of Congress to allow a longer period for amendment, and that Congress alone is the judge of what is a reasonable time. To judge, Congress needs to make "an appraisal of a great variety of relevant conditions, political, social, and economic," and this judgment will naturally vary with the times and with the issue.[32] There is nothing which would constrain Congress to treat a call as lapsing after seven years. Just as Congress formally extended

[29]Gunther, *Op. Cit.*, p. 7.

[30]125 *Cong. Record* at S. 1308 (February 8, 1979).

[31]*Dillon v. Gloss* 256 U.S. 368 (1921) at 375-376.

[32]*Coleman v. Miller* 307 U.S. at 453.

the time for ratifying the Equal Rights Amendment beyond seven years, so it has the discretion to treat the Mississippi request for a Convention as valid after 1982. As economic, political, and social conditions are not substantially different now than they were in 1975, it would be reasonable for Congress to do so.

Addressee. A second point Congress must judge is the validity of calls made to a variety of addressees. Balanced budget calls have been addressed to the President, the Vice President, and various committees of the Congress as well as the Congress itself.[33] The North Dakota call is addressed to no one in particular but simply says that "we . . . call upon the people of the several states for a Convention . . ."[34] Does the addressee, or lack of addressee, affect validity?

Here a commonsense approach is to be preferred. The relevant question is, "Does a state intend to start the amending process under Article V?" If that is the state's intent, the etiquette observed is irrelevant. The Constitution itself is vague as to addressees. It mentions none. It does speak of "the Application of the Legislatures," but although "applications" is a word often used by commentators to describe the individual states' initiatives under Article V, the Constitution itself speaks in the singular, using "Application" only to describe the end product of initiatives or calls of two-thirds of the states.

It is evident from the Constitution that the states must ask in a way that Congress hears. But the Constitution is not a book of manners in the style of Emily Post, Amy Vanderbilt, or Tish Baldrige. The particular addressee is not crucial as long as the message is communicated to Congress.

"Publication in the *Congressional Record,*" one commentator has observed, "serves as a form of official notice that Congress has received the application."[35] Surely there is no

---

[33]Dwight W. Connely, "Amending the Constitution: Is This Any Way to Call for a Constitutional Convention?", *Arizona Law Review* 22 (1980) 4, p. 1031.

[34]125 *Cong. Record* S 1310 (February 8, 1979).

[35]Connely, *Op. Cit.,* p. 1031.

more public way of notifying Congress that a state has voted to ask for a Convention. All the balanced budget calls by the states have in fact been published in the *Congressional Record*.[36] When three more states vote to call and their requests are published in the same journal, "Application" will have been made.

Majorities. The timeliness of a state call and its addressee are essentially procedural questions. A third question of the same kind is the nature of the vote in the state legislature requesting the Convention. It has been observed that the vote in the Colorado Senate for the balanced budget Convention was oral. It has been argued that the lack of a written record is grounds for rejecting the vote because Congress has no basis for determining "the number of Colorado state senators subscribing to the resolution."[37] The implicit assumption in this argument is that Congress must set a minimum, such as an absolute majority of all state senators for a state resolution to be valid. But this assumption and the argument based on it confuse two things—Congress's power to determine validity and a uniform federal rule for all resolutions.

Congress has the power to determine validity,[38] but it is dealing with states which are recognized by the Constitution itself as being, in many respects, distinct sovereignties with the federal union. In petitioning for a Convention, the states are performing a governmental function which, as Madison and Mason indicated, was meant to be substantially free of congressional obstruction. Consequently, it would be counterconstitutional for Congress not to respect the modalities which each state has found appropriate to determine its own legislative will.

Specifically, to take the case of Colorado, if a voice vote satisfies the Colorado legislature as a way of voting on an

---

[36]See Walter E. Dellinger, "The Recurring Question of the 'Limited' Convention," *Yale Law Journal* 88 (1979) 8, p. 1623.

[37]Connely, *Op. Cit.*, p. 1026.

[38]See *Leser v. Garnett* U.S. 130 (1922). (In ratifying an amendment a state performs a federal function).

amendment, there is little to be gained by Congress imposing a different standard. For Colorado, a majority suffices; it does not matter that it is only a majority or a quorum. For Congress to reject this vote would be for Congress to say that a higher majority is needed—a majority of the membership. Congress does not use full membership as the basis for determining the number in Congress required to approve an amendment. It would be unreasonable to impose such a requirement on the fifty states. And it would be profoundly disrespectful to the states to do so.

As for uniformity, sufficient uniformity exists if the federal rule is: A Convention call is valid if it has been adopted by a state legislature in compliance with the rules for valid action by that legislature. Obviously such a simple rule means that an act by one branch of a legislature will not be a valid call. Obviously the rule means that legislatures which can regularly adopt resolutions without gubernatorial approval can do so here. But it also means that some states will act by majority votes and some by higher margins. Congress in its plenary power to pass judgments on validity can and should find both standards valid.

Invalidating content? Beyond procedure, there are questions of content. Two kinds of questions press in particular as concerns the balanced budget calls. Are certain calls to be invalidated because they should be characterized as "conditional?" Are all the calls to be catalogued by the language they employ and only those calls using identical language to be counted together as asking for a Convention on the same subject?

The argument is made by Walter E. Dellinger, Professor of Law at Duke University Law School, that a state call for a Convention for "the sole and exclusive purpose" of proposing a particular amendment is invalid. A substantial number of the calls for a balanced budget Convention are of this character. All are invalid, according to Professor Dellinger. His reason is that they "call only a Convention shackled by constraints that Congress has no power to impose, and they expressly or by implication oppose the calling of a Convention on any other basis."[39] In other words, these calls are conditional, and conditional upon terms which cannot be imposed on Congress. The conditions being impossible to meet, the calls themselves fail.

Professor Dellinger's argument is learned and ingenious but shows little trace of common sense. Professor Dellinger seems not disappointed in believing that most legislators are fools doing foolish things which he is sharp enough to point out. He achieves this superiority by being super-technical and ignoring the basic requirements of the Constitution which sets up the popular process of amendment.

The calls for a Convention for the sole and exclusive purpose of proposing a particular form of balanced budget amendment are not to be read with the sharp eye and narrow vision of a conveyancer. They are calls for a Convention on a particular topic—a balanced budget—and not on some other topic such as gun control or nuclear weapons. But they cannot be effectively more specific than the nature of the amending process permits. As virtually everyone, including Professors Black and Gunther, has admitted, a Convention is a deliberative body, not a registry recording documents. Necessarily it will discuss, debate, and ultimately put in final form the amendment it will propose for adoption. As Professor Black stingingly remarks, a Convention to perform a merely ministerial function is "a bit of foolishness one can by no stretch of fancy think the Constitution calls for."[40] But apparently both he and Professor Dellinger think what is beyond the stretch of fancy is what many legislatures have done. Common sense repudiates this interpretation.

Common sense says that the legislatures have called for a balanced budget Convention. Many legislatures have even indicated in strong and peremptory words the exact language they expect such a Convention to adopt. But by the very nature

[39]Dellinger, "Who Controls a Constitutional Convention? — A Response," *Duke Law Journal* (1974) 4, p. 1001.

[40]Black, *Op. Cit.*, p. 644.

of a Convention, it cannot be confined to mere mechanical recording of the language of the call. Limited to a particular topic by "the Application" of the states and the terms set by Congress, any Convention will be able to write the precise language of the amendment on the subject for which it is called. Whatever exhortations or conditions precedent or conditions subsequent the states insert, when they ask for a Convention they ask for a body with this degree of flexibility.

The legislature of Delaware in a resolution accompanying its call declares that it "interprets Article V to mean" that a Convention "would not have the power to vary the text" or "to propose other amendments on the same propositions." This statement by the legislature is mere opinion, not a part of its call, and it must be disregarded since the nature of any Convention is such as to require deliberation and drafting. It is a statement which is surplusage, not a condition invalidating the call by Delaware. Similarly the less explicit but analogous attempts of other legislatures to dictate a text must be regarded not as creating invalid conditions but as conveying legislative opinion without binding force.

There is, however, one kind of condition which is not so narrow as to be ineffective. It is the kind adopted by Nevada that "this legislature conditions this request upon the Congress of the United States establishing appropriate restrictions limiting the subject matter of a Convention called pursuant to this resolution to the subject matter of this resolution, and if the Congress fails to establish such restrictions, this resolution has no effect and must be considered a nullity."[41] This condition merely expresses what is the duty of Congress in calling a Convention in response to "the Application" of the legislatures. It cannot go beyond the Application. As Nevada adds nothing to the constitutional duty already incumbent on Congress, this condition is effective and harmless.

In the same way Utah has provided that its call is to be counted "only if the Convention is limited to the subject

<hr />

[41]125 *Cong. Record* S 1309 (February 8, 1979). `

matter of this Resolution;" and North Carolina has provided that its call is to be "deemed rescinded in the event the Convention is not limited to the subject matter of this application."[42] These specifications accomplish what Nevada accomplishes. They restrict Congress to its duty.

Several states, however, have used even more precise and peremptory language. Colorado, for example, after calling for a Convention "for the specific and exclusive purpose of proposing an amendment . . . prohibiting deficit spending," further resolved "that this application and request be deemed null and void, rescinded and of no effect in the event that such Convention not be limited to such specific and exclusive purpose."[43] Idaho called for a Convention with similar language as to nullity and recision if the Convention were not limited "to such specific and exclusive purpose."[44] Resolutions of this kind have furnished Professor Dellinger with ammunition. They ask, he says, for unconstitutionally narrow Conventions—Conventions limited to proposing only the exact text the legislature has approved in its call. Consequently, to use his words, they "simply self-destruct."[45]

These resolutions do self-destruct if Congress fails to limit the Convention to the sole and exclusive purpose of proposing a balanced budget amendment. Such is their intent and design. But they do not self-destruct in the sense meant by Professor Dellinger, who treats them as self-destructive at the very moment of their adoption. His mistake is to read them with a literalism which does violence to their sense and purpose.

Read in a fair way, these resolutions require Congress to call a Convention for the sole and exclusive purpose of proposing a balanced budget amendment. They are limitations on the subject not the verbatim text. They ask in substance what the

---

[42]124 *Cong. Record* S 2363 (March 8, 1979) and S 1123 (February 6, 1979).

[43]*Ibid.,* S 1306 (February 8, 1979).

[44]*Ibid.,* S 1932 (March 1, 1979).

[45]Dellinger, "The Recurring Questions," p. 1638.

resolutions of North Carolina and Utah ask. Professor Dellinger admits as much for he treats them alike as invalid.[46] But the North Carolina and Utah limitations are valid. It would put too much weight on technical words to say that Colorado and Idaho have acted invalidly because they used a different formula. We are not construing real property law or eighteenth century codes of pleading. When in substance what is clear is a demand for subject limitations, the exact words chosen should not be pressed to the point that the basic request is destroyed.

Similarity of subject. How close in content do the calls have to be in order for them to be on the same subject? The question in a sense has been answered by the foregoing discussion. The states are asking Congress to call a Convention, not register a document. The calls are close enough because a reasonable person will have no difficulty in saying that they deal with the same matter.

Florida has asked Congress to call a Convention "for the sole purpose of proposing an amendment to the Constitution of the United States to require a balanced federal budget and to make certain exceptions with respect thereto."[47] Georgia, Iowa, Louisiana, New Hampshire, and Oregon have used virtually identical language, as has North Carolina except that it refers to a balanced budget "in the absence of a national emergency." The slight variations in the text produce no change in the subject.

Alabama has asked for a Convention "for the specific and exclusive purpose of proposing an amendment to the Federal Constitution requiring in the absence of a national emergency that the total of all federal appropriations made by the Congress for any fiscal year may not exceed the total of all estimated revenues for that fiscal year."[48] Similar calls have been made by Alaska, Arizona, Arkansas, Idaho, Indiana, Kansas, Nebraska, Nevada, New Mexico, Oklahoma,

[46]*Ibid.*, pp. 1637-1638.
[47]*Cong. Record* S 1307 (February 8, 1979).
[48]*Ibid.*, S 1306 (February 8, 1979).

Pennsylvania, South Dakota, Texas, Utah, and Virginia. These states agree with each other. No reasonable person would doubt that the language they have used designates the same topic which Florida and her sister states have designated by the phrase "balanced budget."

Several states have been slightly more individual in their wording. Thus Colorado asks for a Convention to propose an amendment "prohibiting deficit spending except under conditions specified in such amendment." Delaware asks consideration of an amendment specifying that "the costs of operating the Federal Government shall not exceed its income during any fiscal year, except in the event of declared war."[49] Maryland and Wyoming add that appropriations may not exceed revenues "excluding any revenues derived from borrowing."[50] Mississippi adds that the national debt shall be repaid and not increased.[51] South Carolina calls for a Convention for "proposing an amendment" and then gives the substantial text in a separate resolution.[52] Tennessee says the amendment is to read "substantially" in a form that it then gives.[53]

Any trained legal observer will pick up these differences in form and expression. They do not establish any substantial differences as to the subject with one exception. Mississippi has added the subject of reduction of the national debt. This is a second and different subject in which the other states have expressed no interest. Mississippi's call here has not been seconded. But its call for a Convention on debt reduction is not integral to its call for a Convention on a balanced budget. It may be safely disregarded without impugning the effectiveness of Mississippi's call for a balanced budget amendment.

It is true that there is a variation as to the exceptions the states propose, of which the greatest variant is the Delaware

[49] *Ibid.*, S 1307 (February 8, 1979).

[50] *Ibid.*, S 1308 and S 1313 (February 8, 1979).

[51] *Ibid.*, S 1308 (February 8, 1979).

[52] *Ibid.*, S 1311 (February 8, 1979).

[53] *Ibid.*, S 1312 (February 8, 1979).

proposal limiting the exception to "the event of declared War." Clearly everyone recognizes that it is impossible to make a balanced budget requirement so absolute that it has no exceptions. Just as clearly the extent of the exceptions are precisely what a Convention would have to determine. Variation in the exceptions offered creates no change in the subject matter of the calls.

In summary, any reasonable person reading the thirty-one calls of the states would observe the difference in style, in form, in emphasis and exception which are entirely expectable when the people of the different states express themselves. But unless the reasonable person were to change into a Scrooge-like scrivener, he or she would have not the slightest trouble in perceiving that all thirty-one states are deeply troubled by deficit federal financing and all thirty-one states ask for a Convention which will provide an amendment mandating a balanced budget as a federal norm. Congress, being composed of reasonable men and women familiar with political processes, will have no trouble in concluding that it has before it thirty-one valid calls for a balanced budget Convention.

Conclusion

A decade after the Constitution had been in operation, Thomas Jefferson wrote, "I wish it were possible to obtain a single amendment to our Constitution. I would be willing to depend on that alone for the reduction of the administration of our government to the genuine principles of its Constitution; I mean an additional article, taking from the federal government the power of borrowing."[54] Jefferson's "single amendment" is the balanced budget amendment. In Jefferson's view, its enactment was necessary to bring the "administration of our government" back to the "genuine principles" of the Constitu-

---

[54]Paul L. Ford, ed., *The Writings of Thomas Jefferson* (New York, 1896), Vol. 7, p. 310. (Jefferson to John Taylor, November 26, 1798).

tion. It's enactment is necessary now to restore the genuine principles of the Constitution.

Article V has given the people of the United States two ways of amending their Constitution. The second is of particular value when Congress has motivation not to use the first. Now, when there is wide popular demand for a balanced federal budget, thirty-one states have wisely and validly invoked the second way. When three more states join their sister-states' call, Congress will be under a preemptory duty to call a Convention limited to consideration of an amendment directed to balancing the budget.[55]

---

[55]See Alexander Hamilton, *The Federalist No. 85, Op. Cit.*, p. 546.

APPENDIX

The Count on The 31 State Legislatures Which Have Passed A Resolution Calling for A Constitutional Convention on A Balanced Federal Budget Amendment

The 31 state legislatures which have passed balanced budget amendment resolutions are:

Alabama	HJR 227, Act 302	1976
Alaska	HJR 17	1982
Arizona	SJR 1002, HCM 2003	1979, 1977
Arkansas	HJR 1	1979
Colorado	SJM 1	1978
Delaware	HCR 36	1975
Florida	Sen. Mem. #234, HM 2801	1976, 1976
Georgia	Res. Act #93, HR #469-1267	1976
Idaho	HCR 7	1979
Indiana	SJR 8	1979
Iowa	SJR 1	1979
Kansas	SCR 1661	1978
Louisiana	SCR 4, SR 73, HCR 269	1979, 1978 1975
Maryland	SJR 4§, Md JR 77*	1975
Mississippi	HCR 51	1975
Nebraska	LR 106	1976
Nevada	SJR 8, SJR 2	1979, 1977
New Hampshire	HCR 8	1979
New Mexico	SJR 1	1976
North Carolina	Resolution 5	1979
North Dakota	SCR 4018	1975
Oklahoma	HJR 1049	1976
Oregon	SJ Mem #2	1977
Pennsylvania	HR 236	1976
South Carolina	SCR 1024, SCR 670	1978, 1976
South Dakota	SJR 1	1979
Tennessee	HJR22	1977
Texas	HCR 13, HCR 31	1978, 1977
Utah	HJR 12	1979
Virginia	SJR 36	1976
Wyoming	HJR 12§, JR 1*	1977

Certified copies of these resolutions are on file at the National Taxpayers Union, 711 Maryland Ave., NE, Washington, DC 20002

§Original
*Enrolled